PSYCHIC VISION

About the Author

Melanie Barnum (Bethel, CT) is a psychic medium, intuitive counselor, life coach, and hypnotist who has been practicing professionally for more than fifteen years. She was a VIP Reader at Psych Out, a gathering of the nation's foremost psychics, organized by Court TV. Barnum is also an Angelspeake Facilitator, a Remote Viewer, and a member of the National Guild of Hypnotists (NGH) and the International Association of Counselors and Therapists (IACT). Visit her online at MelanieBarnum.com.

MELANIE BARNUM

PSYCHIC VISION

DEVELOPING YOUR CLAIRVOYANT AND REMOTE VIEWING SKILLS

Llewellyn Publications
Woodbury, Minnesota

First Edition
Second Printing, 2015

Cover art: iStockphoto.com/38680434/©Nastco
iStockphoto.com/20986828/©Xavier Arnau
iStockphoto.com/47209912/©sumkinn
Shutterstock/59123398/©Zffoto
Shutterstock/125853965/©Mykola Mazuryk
Shutterstock/45010153/©Timofeyev Alexander
Shutterstock/151627997/©Zacarias Pereira da Mata
Shutterstock/148797470/©Evelyn Sugar
Shutterstock/214405087/©mythja
Cover design: Kevin R. Brown
Interior Illustrations: Llewellyn Art Department

Llewellyn Publishing is a registered trademark of Llewellyn Worldwide Ltd.

Library of Congress Cataloging-in-Publication Data

Barnum, Melanie, 1969–
Psychic vision : developing your clairvoyant & remote viewing skills /
Melanie Barnum. — First Edition.
    pages cm
Includes bibliographical references and index.
ISBN 978-0-7387-4623-4
1. Clairvoyance. 2. Remote viewing (Parapsychology) I. Title.
BF1325.B34 2015
133.8'4—dc23
                    2015013847

Llewellyn Worldwide Ltd. does not participate in, endorse, or have any authority or responsibility concerning private business transactions between our authors and the public.

All mail addressed to the author is forwarded, but the publisher cannot, unless specifically instructed by the author, give out an address or phone number.

Any Internet references contained in this work are current at publication time, but the publisher cannot guarantee that a specific location will continue to be maintained. Please refer to the publisher's website for links to authors' websites and other sources.

Llewellyn Publications
A Division of Llewellyn Worldwide Ltd.
2143 Wooddale Drive
Woodbury, MN 55125-2989
www.llewellyn.com

Printed in the United States of America

Other Books by Melanie Barnum

The Book of Psychic Symbols

The Steady Way to Greatness

Psychic Abilities for Beginners

This book is dedicated to my family:
Tom, Molly, and Samantha.

Without their continued support it would never have been
written. Their pride shines through every time they ask if they
can give their teachers one of my books or their friends ask me
to help them understand.

Thank you so much ~ for being you!

Acknowledgments

With every book I've written I can't help but thank all of the professional psychics and authors who have come before me and will continue after me. It is incredible to think that this subject matter, which has been taboo for so long, is becoming so mainstream. It is through these pioneers that I am able to continue doing what I love and what I consider a major part of my life's purpose.

None of this would have been possible without the hard work of everyone at Llewellyn, especially Angela Wix. Your dedication has at times both challenged and encouraged me. Thank you!

My sister, Tammy, who continues to believe in my own greatness and insight, has been one of my greatest champions and believes in me even when I don't. And my friends. They've been there for me throughout the ups and downs of my deadlines and my events, cheering me on and raising me up. Kathy has been there, encouraging and even challenging me to be the best psychic and author I can be, even though she's "the psychic one." I'm also very excited to think my "BFFN" is slowly coming around, and my "satellite office roommate," with the helpful addition of the random words that she'd throw at me until they stuck, has helped me finish!

To all of my clients who've come to me for help and those who have shared their personal stories through this book, I thank you! Your gratitude is more than appreciated, because without you I wouldn't be able to do this work and continue to learn—it really is you who help me! Finally, and probably most importantly, thanks to my helpers on the other side! To my mother, who helps me with every single reading. Though I can't have you here with me physically, I am ecstatic you are with me in spirit. It is my mom, along with all of my other deceased loved ones, my guides, and my angels, assists me in communicating with all of the spiritual helpers my clients bring with them who allow me to do what I love!

To everyone who is reading this right now—thank you! Enjoy!

Contents

Part One
Psychic Vision—Clairvoyance

Part Two
Coordinate Remote Viewing

Part Three
Practice & Practical Use

Editor's Note

The practices and techniques described in this book should not be used as an alternative to professional medical treatment. This book does not attempt to give medical diagnoses, treatment, prescriptions, or suggestions for medication in relation to any human disease, pain, injury, deformity, or physical or mental condition.

The author and publisher of this book are not responsible in any manner whatsoever for any injury that may occur through following the examples contained herein. It is recommended that you consult your physician to obtain a diagnosis for any physical or mental symptoms you may experience.

Author's Note Regarding
Coordinate Remote Viewing

The methods and format used to describe and teach Coordinate Remote Viewing (CRV) in this book are derived from the *Coordinate Remote Viewing Training Manual*, originally created, assembled, and documented by the Stanford Research Institute International through a coordinated effort with physicists Russell Targ, PhD; Harold Puthoff, PhD; artist and psychic Ingo Swann; and retired Army General Paul Smith, as well as the Defense Intelligence Agency (DIA). Paul Smith, who strenuously resisted making the CRV manual public, states this manual was created as a way to preserve the methodology of Ingo Swann, and in part as "a guide for future training purposes" (Gaenir, *The Coordinate Remote Viewing Manual*). This manual has been reprinted in various formats for training purposes, explanation purposes, and literary purposes, and can be located freely on the Internet through a variety of websites. In some locations it is listed to be the copyrighted property of Ingo Swann, although in a detailed conversation between Ingo Swann and Palyne "PJ" Gaenir, Swann claims to never have written such a document (Gaenir, *The Coordinate Remote Viewing Manual*).

The methods and descriptions in this book are also derived from the author's own personal training and experiences during and after earning her certification as a Coordinate Remote Viewer. The charts and procedures are based on the original trainings and documents received by the author to be used to perform remote viewing sessions and to teach others to remote view. The practices and exercises contained herein do not in any way equal or replace the training the original viewers received. For anyone serious about performing advanced remote viewing, the author suggests seeking additional training and practice, preferably with someone from the governmental program.

"We only have to exert our minds a little more than usual to awaken our psychic vision."

—James Van Praagh

Introduction

Who Am I?

Are you ready for change? Good! I've got a secret and I want to share it with you. I want you to know things that I know and experience some of what I experience. But who am I? Well, that's a very interesting question. It depends on the day or the hour or even the moment that you ask. I'm a mother, a friend, a wife, a sister, and a daughter. I'm an average person like most of the population on this earth. Oh, and by the way, I'm a psychic.

I wasn't always known as "the psychic" around town. That didn't happen until more recently, after I published my first book a few years ago. Then the secret was out. Those who didn't know now did, and those who had already known let out a sigh of relief, like it was some sort of secret burden they had been carrying. My office, you see, is not in my hometown, and most of my clients come to me by word of mouth or through my website from all over the world. Even though I've been a practicing psychic offering individual and group readings for the better part of two decades, most people in my neighborhood knew me as a cheer coach or lacrosse mom of two wonderful girls. Little did they know that I am *also* the psychic around town.

It's not like I grew up talking to dead people. I really didn't see deceased loved ones or receive messages of doom or encouragement whispered in my ears. I was a normal, pretty well-adjusted kid with an older sister and brother and a single-parent mother who was my best friend.

Luckily for me, I was not hit by lightning, and I didn't die and come back to life. My awakening to this enhanced psychic ability instead stemmed from a knowing—a feeling of being hit over the head with a psychic club—and I heard the words *You need to do this now*. When that happened, almost twenty years ago, I knew immediately that the universe had conspired in deciding it was about time I tune in to the other side and develop my psychic gifts.

Though I knew I had to do it—after all, there's not much of an argument available to you when the universe says "jump"—I didn't quite agree with the timeline. I mean, really, what did *You need to do this now* actually imply? That I close down the store I had just built from scratch, or hang a shingle that said "psychic" outside my door? Come on. I was a rational, intelligent person. I was an accountant, for Pete's sake, a former controller of a large company. This just seemed like a preposterous idea and I knew I needed to have more than a giant paranormal hand with a bat swaying me; I needed credentials.

So, recognizing I had to work some psychic triage to decide how serious or in-depth I had to go with each divining skill and with which intuitive abilities, as well as which should come first, I set out to learn what my new career would entail. I began studying and taking certification courses in all types of personal healing and paranormal areas. I started with the basics. I had a reading with an angel reader, Trudy Griswold, who, together with her sister Barbara Mark, had published a series of Angelspeake books. That reading propelled me to take her weeklong course and become a Certified Angelspeake Facilitator. (According to the books they'd written, an Angelspeake Facilitator is someone who teaches you how to communicate with angels in a specific way, using automatic writing.) Once again, God and the universe had joined forces in pushing me into the right place at the right time, and so began my journey. I continued to study with teachers known worldwide, as well as those whose names would probably not be recognized by more than a handful of people.

Still not feeling one hundred percent confident in my newly uncovered abilities, I started off by giving free readings to hundreds of people over the Internet. Simple ones, usually, at times a single question and other times a more in-depth but basic session. Offering psychic insight to people all over the world helped me to hone my craft without worrying I wasn't performing. As my gifts increased, I realized people who shared something of value usually rated the information in my reading for them more significantly. That was when I was ready to begin my professional career, which meant I was ready to hang that shingle and start charging for my intuitive services.

Feeling tuned in, I knew my psychic abilities were increasing with every reading, but I still felt something was missing. Being very logical, I decided I also needed to feed my left brain, or my rational side. Training in mostly right-brained work such as intuition, random thought, and creativity had helped me connect to my psychic side, but I wanted science to back up what I was learning.

This led me to dive into training with a retired United States Army major who had been an original member of the government's psychic spy training program, which was eventually named Stargate. It was a top-secret, scientifically driven program with specific protocol and rigid methods known as Coordinate Remote Viewing (CRV), or seeing persons, places, and things distant in time and space. This helped me understand the basis for what I was doing even though the procedure was entirely different. It fulfilled and satisfied the need to work with both the right, creative side of my brain, and the left, logical side.

I now read for people near and far, who are all looking for answers, out of my Ridgefield, Connecticut, office and over the phone and Internet. These people are hoping for guidance with some of the most basic aspects of life: family, love, finances, career, health, and overall happiness. These themes are consistent regardless of what country they're in, though the content is never the same from one person to another. I've learned over my many years of being a professional psychic intuitive and medium (have I said I talk to dead people?) that this is definitely what I am meant to do. While I questioned the importance of this work as it first was not-so-gently suggested to me, I have come to truly love what I do. It is said you will never work a day in your life if you enjoy it. Almost twenty years since I began my journey, I am extremely happy to have been metaphysically hit over the head and told it was time to start pursuing what I believe to be my life's purpose. My ability to share information with people psychically, intuitively, and clairvoyantly to help them has been one of my greatest accomplishments.

Why This Book?

Now that you know who I am, it's time to discover who you are! Of course, you know yourself already, but have you tuned in to your *clairvoyance*? Clairvoyance means "clear vision," "clear" being from the French *clair*. This book will not only tell you what remote viewing is (from psychic vision to CRV as used by various governments), but will give you an opportunity to practice it as well. If you are interested in psychic development, intuition, hidden practices, psychic espionage, conspiracy theories, government programs, or simply want to learn techniques to find lost items, this book is for you!

If you've chosen this book, congratulate yourself! You've just taken a huge step toward tuning in to your psychic abilities. Clairvoyance is a huge part of intuitive development. Eighteenth-century French physician and philosopher Julien Offray de La Mettrie said, "Everyone is born with psychic abilities. It's just a matter of knowing how to tap into it" (www.quotesdaddy.com/quote/1130894/mettrie-l/everyone-is-born-with-psychic-abilities-its-just and http://www.famousquotesabout.com/quote/Everyone-is-born-with/404568). Being confident in your stages of development may not always feel natural, but it is my hope that you will learn to not only accept your role but also embrace the incredible joy and fun you will have along the way.

Before you read this book, and hopefully learn some new concepts, it's a good idea to explore clairvoyance and Coordinate Remote Viewing and what they mean to you. Learning how you identify with what you're reading is made easier by using the *Try It Now!* sections located throughout every chapter. Discovering what you already know about psychic vision is your first one!

Try It Now!

What Do I Know?

Get yourself a journal that can be used throughout the entire book for exercises as well as any notes you may have. When you are done with all of the exercises in this book, you may find it to be an invaluable resource for your future endeavors. Take out your journal and a pencil and jump right in to your first exercise. Write down your answers to the following questions.

- Have you ever heard of the terms *psychic vision* or *clairvoyance?*
- Have you ever heard of remote viewing?
- What would your definitions be of each of these terms?
- Have you ever had any personal experiences with psychic vision or remote viewing?
- Do you believe it's possible to possess some type of intuition or psychic ability?
- Do you believe you have some intuitive ability?
- What are some of your favorite activities or hobbies?
- Does your idea of a fun evening include reading this book, practicing your clairvoyance, or some other form of psychic play, either alone or with friends?
- Do you believe you can view things distant in time and space?
- Do you think governments may have researched psychic phenomena?

~If you've answered yes to any of these questions or listed anything related to psychic play, remote viewing, or intuition as any of your favorite things to do, then you've chosen the right book!

~If you've answered no to most of these questions or haven't listed anything related to psychic ability, then you are on your path to discovering a whole new world to enjoy!

What to Expect from This Book

As you take the time to move from start to finish through all three parts of this book, expect the unexpected! You may, and probably will, discover aspects of yourself and your life you may never have known were there. But how will you do this? By learning two distinct forms of vision: clairvoyance and Coordinate Remote Viewing. You will have ample opportunity to practice both forms of viewing. There are numerous exercises throughout the book designed to help you not only understand but also become more proficient with each type. The more you practice the exercises, the more familiar you will become with your own psychic and remote viewing abilities. You will also discover that by learning both formats you will increase your overall competence with clairvoyance and Coordinate Remote Viewing.

In part one, you will begin to understand exactly what psychic vision is, but that is just the beginning. You will learn all about clairvoyance and how it can enhance your life, but learning about something is not nearly as much fun as actually participating in it. Luckily, you will have ample breaks and exercises to do just that!

As you dive into this part, you will be shown that we don't just use our physical eyes to see. We are able to see even with our eyes closed by using our third eye, or our psychic eye. Utilizing this gift allows us to reach out to the other side and receive messages from our loved ones in spirit and our guides, commonly known as mediumship. Any time you connect to your psychic abilities, you are being a conduit or a medium to the energies on the other side. Your psychic gifts will also assist you in making decisions and discerning between a good or positive situation and one that will have a negative outcome.

Learning to recognize when you are experiencing a clairvoyant moment is imperative to acting on your psychic visions, and this section of the book will help you become aware of those times. Through practice and exercises you will become more cognizant of how clairvoyance feels and appears for you personally, as each individual has a common yet unique way of tuning in to his or her psychic sight. Assisted by the many shared stories of true psychic visions and readings, you will easily identify how clairvoyance can become part of everyone's life. Through the examples, you will also learn how every aspect of your intuition often contributes to your clairvoyant abilities, and you will discover which of these gifts resonates with you more.

Later in this section, your clairvoyant and physical eyes will be opened to the ever-present realities of symbols, signs, and synchronicities and how they show up in your daily life. You will learn that without recognizing symbols, the psychic visions you may have can be jumbled and disconcerting at best. You will also allow yourself to become immersed in an ever-increasing world where a coincidence is no longer merely coincidence, but instead, more often than not, contains a hidden or deeper meaning.

All in all, in part one you will become attuned to your own clairvoyance, regardless of the level of natural ability you may have. You will come to understand how psychic sight is used to access your mediumistic gifts, have premonitory visions, and see objects or people in distant locations as well as images that answer questions you may have. This section will explainwhen psychic vision can help you and how you can recognize it amidst any cloud of distrust or confusion. It will also afford you the opportunity to begin creating an amazing journal you can use as a reference guide or merely as a personal diary as you traverse through this eye-opening book, designed to not only instruct you on psychic sight, but also possibly even create a love for your newly found or unearthed gifts.

As you move into part two, you'll discover the differences between using your psychic sight versus the governmentally developed program

Coordinate Remote Viewing. Unlike clairvoyance, Coordinate Remote Viewing developers have created a very specific protocol to see things distant in time and space without the necessity of possessing any type of psychic ability whatsoever. By following the procedures laid out step by step, you will learn how to tap into this highly coveted, formerly classified method of remote viewing. You will be privy to the same methods the United States government has admitted to using to train agents and military personnel in psychic espionage.

Through the use of simplified physics, you will learn how to tune in to the subject line to pick up details of what you are trying to view. You will be given multiple opportunities to practice it for yourself with the various targets provided. Each exercise will take you further into the target data, exposing you to methods previously unavailable to the layperson or even the most accomplished psychic. Understanding how to distinguish between remote viewing and regular vision is made easier with each practice session.

Although you can easily skip part one and jump directly into part two to delve into the somewhat clandestine world of Coordinate Remote Viewing, you may find yourself wanting to go back and discover the not-so-secret world of psychic vision or clairvoyance. Either way works—reading part one or part two first is totally up to you. Written as two very distinct parts, they are two different approaches to seeing the world beyond what is in front of you; there is more out there than what appears to the naked eye.

In part three, you will get even deeper into the practice and personal use of these techniques and abilities. Discovering when and where to use clairvoyance is an important part of being prudent as well as responsible, which is discussed in this last section. Understanding why it's not always the time or place to utilize your clairvoyance can keep you from overstepping your boundaries with others. Knowing when to utilize your remote viewing versus your psychic vision can also allow you to obtain a greater awareness than you may have had using the alternative method. The two methods are different, indeed, but can produce many of the same ultimate results when necessary. Part three also shares how group remote viewing can allow for multiple perspectives of the same thing, and there is ample opportunity to become skilled at how to work together in the group viewing and sample targets chapters.

Finally, understanding how the process can help you and the benefits of tuning in and using your very own psychic and remote viewing abilities will present you with a whole new way of looking at life, and maybe even death. It will help you expose and uncover secrets and ideas you may have never been privy to. Discovering how to utilize your psychic gifts and learning the process of Coordinate Remote Viewing can help you with everything from answering your own personal question of whether you will get a job to helping find a missing person.

It is up to you to begin your new journey into expanded vision and to make yourself so much better than the magnificent being you already are. You, that's right, you! You are a unique individual and you have the opportunity to evoke change for yourself and in your environment. And you are so lucky to have one of the greatest tools in your tool belt to do that: knowledge. As someone once said, "Be the change you wish to see in the world" (Unknown). So, get ready and strap in—it's time to enjoy this visionary ride!

Part One

PSYCHIC VISION— CLAIRVOYANCE

"Vision is the art of seeing what is invisible to others."
—Jonathan Swift

Chapter One
What Is Psychic Vision?

What is psychic vision? It is exactly what it sounds like. It is the ability to see beyond normal physical sight, using extrasensory perception and seeing with your mind's eye, internally. It's an incredible gift that comes naturally to some, but for all can be developed with practice. Imagine the endless possibilities if you were able to psychically view which path to take, or which car would outlast the rest, or even where the blockage was in someone's bloodstream. The sky's the limit; the amount of information obtainable to you would be exponential in its availability. There's an infinite amount of possibilities.

Psychic sight, commonly known as clairvoyance, conjures up a myriad of images, including those of boardwalk gypsies and charlatans whose only desire is to take as much money as possible out of your wallet. Thankfully, this perception has lessened over the years, but it's still there for those who haven't had any experience with it themselves or who haven't witnessed the phenomenon of anything paranormal. Clairvoyance for many is an untapped gift waiting to be utilized.

Receiving information from the other side, also referred to as our deceased loved ones, spirit guides, angels, the universe, or even God, is normal. I am a practicing psychic, someone who communicates with the unearthly plane in order to bring messages and healing to those who are here. Clairvoyance is one of the most common ways to perceive this information.

We are given images from our guides and other helpers to assist us in understanding their messages to us. Clairvoyance is an ordinary and practical way to obtain those intuitive communications. We have something called a third eye, or our sixth chakra. Chakras are metaphysical energy centers, or spinning wheels of energy, often referred to as spiritual batteries. We have seven that travel up the body along the spine. No, we are not Cyclopes, but our third eye *is* located in the center of the forehead above the brow line. However, it is an energy center, not a physical eyeball. It is with this clairvoyant chakra that we psychically see.

Some people experience psychic visions as flashes of color or light. Other times the messages come through like Polaroid pictures or still images, in either black-and-white or full color. Occasionally, it will be like watching a movie playing in your mind. One of the most difficult obstacles to get past is determining whether what you're seeing is truly a psychic message or merely your imagination. This is why so many impressions are discounted as nothing or as not being real.

Getting past that barrier of disbelief and trusting that there is more to view than what the naked eye can see may take some time. Believe it or not, utilizing your imagination can actually help you recognize when you are experiencing psychic sight. Proving to yourself that there is indeed another layer of vision of paranormal sight available to you can change everything you believe. Learning how to use your imagination is paramount to that belief. Being able to see in your mind what your imagination is showing you opens you to being able to see psychically in your mind.

Try It Now!

Imagine This!

You're going to tune in to your own imagination. Close your eyes. Using your imagination, see in your mind's eye a beautiful white gazebo. Envision the gazebo with six sides and a round, pointed roof. Imagine there is a bench that runs the whole perimeter of the inside except where the opening is to enter and exit.

Now, imagine that when you look beyond the gazebo you are seeing a beautiful green field, and spread out around the field there are wildflowers. Imagine you can see orange poppies, yellow daffodils, white daisies, purple irises, blue hydrangeas, pink tulips, and red roses. As you look toward the sky, imagine you can see the beautiful blue broken only by bits of white clouds as fluffy as cotton candy at a carnival.

While you're visualizing the beauty all around you, look down at your feet. Imagine you are standing on grass so lush it's like standing on a green cushion of air. Now, take a last look around and really see all of the colors; see the crispness of every petal and each blade of grass. Imagine the yellow sun as it bounces off the brilliant white gazebo.

Allow yourself the luxury of relaxing for a bit in this incredible place. When you are ready, open your eyes.

Now check yes or no:

	Yes	No
Did you see the gazebo?	❏	❏
Did you count the sides?	❏	❏
Did you see the roof?	❏	❏
Did you see the opening?	❏	❏
Did you see the green field?	❏	❏
Did you see the colors of the flowers?	❏	❏
Orange?	❏	❏
Yellow?	❏	❏
White?	❏	❏
Purple?	❏	❏
Blue?	❏	❏
Pink?	❏	❏

Red?	❑	❑
Did you see the blue sky?	❑	❑
Did you see the white fluffy clouds?	❑	❑
Did you see the green grass?	❑	❑
Did you see the yellow sun?	❑	❑

If you answered yes to all of them, hooray! You're able to see in your mind's eye. That's one step closer to tapping into your clairvoyant abilities. If you answered yes to half of them, great! You're open to psychic visions. With practice you'll be able to see them even more clearly. If you answered no to all of them, that's okay. Don't worry. There are plenty of opportunities to practice throughout the rest of the book.

Seeing Things

"Why am I drawing this?" I asked Jeannette as I doodled a swirly, shell-like picture on the paper in front of me. I was sitting at my antique mahogany desk in my office, with my client opposite me. The only thing separating us was a mere twenty inches of wood, but in reality there was a whole dimension. I was doing a reading for her and I had been connecting to the other side for the previous forty-five minutes when this image came to mind. The only way to describe it was to draw it.

"What the... oh my God! Where did you come up with that?" Jeannette asked incredulously.

"I just saw it in my mind and knew I had to show it to you. Why? It feels kind of important in some way," I replied.

I had been tuning in to her deceased mother, giving her evidence through my psychic communication that her mother was still around and sending her love every day. I had also told Jeanette her mother was aware of everything she was doing. I had just mentioned her father immediately before seeing the spiral illustration with my intuition.

"Yeah, it's a big deal all right! It represents so much!" She could barely contain her amazement.

"Well, what does it mean? Don't leave me in suspense!" I countered.

"Just everything to do with my father and his wife, my stepmother!"

Jeannette went on to explain it was the *koru* symbol for people who live in New Zealand (who are also known as *Kiwi*), which is where her father now lives. It symbolizes new beginnings. On an even more personal level, it is the name of her father's boat and it was on all of their wedding accoutrements. They had also given everyone necklaces and cuff links with the koru symbol. Obviously, the fact that I saw this image psychically meant everything to her. It let her know that her mother was aware of the wedding during which her father had remarried.

Although I had been tuning in to her energy, psychically, for the better part of an hour and telling her things that I was receiving through my extrasensory perception, it was this symbol that I saw using my clairvoyance that provided her with her "aha" moment. It was that spiral that proved beyond a shadow of a doubt that her mother was indeed around and had witnessed the marriage to the new wife. And while my client knew me to be a professional with the utmost integrity during my readings, this made her just about jump out of her chair. She knew without reservation that what I was seeing was real and was connected to the other side. Jeannette understood that beyond all logic, I saw this to bring her comfort and the healing that she needed.

Try It Now!

Visualize It!

Being able to visualize something in your mind without having it physically in front of you is crucial to using your clairvoyance. Whether you are, like me, aware that you are tuning in to your psychic sight through mediumship or you are just trying to see an answer to a question or a direction, visualization is key to the recognition of what you are clairvoyantly seeing. The ability to draw from your own memories or imagination can help you in accessing your clairvoyant gifts.

Try to see the symbol I saw by using your imagination. Close your eyes and take a few deep breaths. While continuing to steadily breathe in and out, let your mind's eye free. You may notice you can still see light or even darkness with your eyes closed. Detect if you see anything else. If so, that's not a problem; let the image fade. That's great.

Now, take it further and begin a spiral shape in your mind's eye. Imagine it's growing and spinning like a hypnotic trance spiral. Allow it to be white, then black, and then green.

When you are done, open your eyes. Then answer each of the following questions one by one and check off yes or no as they apply to what you just experienced.

	Yes	No
Did you see anything when you closed your eyes?	❏	❏
If so, were you able to let it fade?	❏	❏
Was it light or dark when you closed your eyes?	❏	❏
Were you able to see the spiral?	❏	❏
Were you able to see it in white?	❏	❏
Were you able to see it in black?	❏	❏
Were you able to see it in green?	❏	❏
Did it feel natural or normal?	❏	❏

If you answered yes to all of these questions, yahoo! You're very visual. If you answered no to half, great! You are on your way. If you answered no to all, it would be a great idea to try again. Relax your mind and give yourself longer to do the exercise. If it still doesn't happen, wait until you are very tired and are about to go to bed, then look for the spiral.

Seeing Beyond

We all come into this world with the ability to see remotely. It's an intrinsic facility we are blessed with when we are born. Usually, we don't discard it intentionally, but often, we do lose it. We've become increasingly dependent upon technology and our normal verbal exchanges, so much so that we ignore our clairvoyant flashes for the more tangible messages. "Today modern communications are so sophisticated, and our social laws and practices so stylized, that few people pay any attention at all to innate clairvoyant ability," said author and psychic William H. Hewitt in his book *Psychic Development for Beginners* (Hewitt, 1996).

There are many instances where we feel embarrassed or even ridiculed into hiding our ability to see remotely. Think of a time when you were in school. Many teachers are pretty receptive and open to the ideas and thoughts we express, but most have to follow a previously created agenda in order to teach what needs to be taught in their curriculum. They don't generally have time for your intuitive musings or psychic discussions. Perhaps, even, they don't want to hear about what you think might be or might happen. Teachers sometimes tune out your ramblings about places you've never been but seem to recognize, not necessarily by choice, but rather out of necessity. They can't grade you on what you clairvoyantly see; they need concrete evidence of what's true. This basic education, by design, shuts down our intuitive core, making it more difficult to expose your intuitive images.

Take it a step further and bring your psychic flashes closer to home. Telling your parents or family that you see one of them losing their job or even someone dying can make even those closest to you afraid, which can cause them to push you away. That alone is enough to shut it down. Or, trying to convince your friends that going to the biggest party of the year is not going to end up well. It's even harder when you can't prove it. After all, if you don't go, how can there be a bad ending? Not having any tangible proof causes you to question your gifts.

And think about it: After a while you stop paying attention to the messages you receive, you stop recognizing them, and they just naturally disappear. You unlearn how to understand them and you don't even notice them anymore. You no longer tap into your clairvoyance. You have no desire to utilize your clairvoyance. You let things happen as they do, letting the chips fall where they may, possibly even still holding onto the belief that everything happens for a reason, so whatever.

But what if you remembered again? What if you discovered you really were an intuitive being beyond all else? What if you started believing you actually had the ability you were born with to see things remotely? How incredible would that be? Psychic, teacher, and author Sonia Choquette reminds us: "Get started on your path by accepting the fact that you're indeed naturally intuitive, even if your sixth sense isn't up and running to its full potential just yet" (Choquette, 2004).

Though we regularly have intuitive flashes, more often than not they are discarded. Usually this is fine and doesn't cause too much chaos, but sometimes these messages are critical. Not taking into consideration the psychic impressions we receive can occasionally have grave repercussions.

"Wow! Why'd you swerve like that?" I asked my husband. We were driving to one of our daughter's many lacrosse games. As we were coming in to a blind corner, he swerved all the way to the right, hugging the side of the road.

"I don't know. It was weird. I saw a car coming toward us on the other side of the road crossing the line and crashing into us. It was so vivid I saw us hitting the guardrail," Tom answered, perplexed.

"Well, I sure am glad you paid attention to your clairvoyance! That was a close one!" I confirmed what he was already thinking.

As we had come around the corner there was indeed a car swerving into our lane. There was a guy driving while texting and he had been looking down at his phone. By the time he saw us and corrected his course he was well into our previous path. If my husband hadn't heeded his psychic warning we would have been in for a very long day, to say the least, and possibly even a devastating, life-changing event.

Thankfully he recognized what he remotely saw and (more importantly) acted on it, so we continued driving and made it to our game without incident. These are the extremes, the "if you don't admit to what you're seeing something really bad will happen" kind of occurrences. Learning to trust them when they happen is almost more important than receiving them in the first place. After all, if you don't acknowledge them, what good does having the psychic vision do you?

Try It Now!

See Past Clairvoyant Experiences

Grab your journal and open it to a fresh page. You are free to answer the following questions quickly, but you may want to take a little time to really think about your answers. Dive into the questions with an open mind!

+ Have you experienced something you thought was an intuitive vision?

+ Did you act on it? If so, did acting on it help you? In what way did it help?

+ If not, did not acting on it hurt or hinder you? If so, in what way?

+ Have you ever had what you would consider to be a critical psychic vision? Did you acknowledge it as such? If not, did you recognize it later? If so, did you act on it? If so, did it help you? If not, did it hurt you?

Review your answers. What do they tell you about your respect for your clairvoyant gifts? Do you feel you understood any messages you received? Did you do those messages justice? Would it have hindered you if you had not listened? Do you feel you need to change the way you respond? Did you even recognize any messages?

Seeing Lottery Numbers

I can't tell you the number of times I've heard, "If you're so psychic, why don't you ever win the lotto?" You know, I've asked myself that at least once a month! I learned long ago that we are given what we desire if it's for our greater good. This, unfortunately, I have deciphered means that winning the lotto right now is not for my greater good. Ugh. This gift, this clair-voyance, would be much better served by having the funding to offer free readings to everyone, worldwide and in person even, right? That's my thought, but it apparently is not in line with what the universe has planned for me.

That doesn't necessarily hold true for everyone, however. Imagine being able to see the lotto numbers. How incredible would that be? Just about everyone could use some extra income. Learning how to see the future can also include seeing the numbers before they are even picked, which is exactly what Lynn asked me to do when I was doing a phone reading for her.

"I really believe I'm destined to win the lotto. I just know it's sup-posed to happen. I feel it in my bones," Lynn told me during her phone session.

She was the sister of a friend of mine and someone I'd met and liked personally. She lived in Pennsylvania, not my state of Connecticut, so the lottery system was different from mine, but they offered the same types of state-issued games. I wanted to help her, but I'd never been able to pick the lotto numbers before. What would be different this time?

"That would be great!" I replied, knowing full well that I, too, was supposed to win the lotto. (I mean, why not?)

"Okay. I know you're amused and don't believe me, but I'm actually serious," she chuckled, almost pleadingly. "Can you try and give me the numbers?" she continued.

"I don't usually do it, and when I do I'm usually not right," I told her in no uncertain terms. "But if I do, you know the rules, right?" I laughed back.

"No, what do you mean?" she asked.

"I mean if I give you the numbers and you win, I get fifty percent!" I exclaimed.

"Hmmm. Well, maybe twenty percent," she joked. "Whatever, just give me those numbers!"

"All right, here goes. I'm not getting the actual lotto numbers, though. I think I'm picking up the Play4," I explained.

"Okay, go for it. I'm writing them down now," Lynn answered.

"Let's see. I'm seeing the numbers 3, 2, and 7," I told her. I had seen the numbers clairvoyantly, as if they were popping up on the ping-pong balls out of the machine.

"Got it. That's only three numbers though. Do you have another one?" she asked.

"I'm only getting three numbers. You need to add the fourth. Even if you have to play all ten possibilities, just add the last number and you'll be good!" I told her.

"Sounds like a plan! I will let you know!"

A couple days later I talked to her sister. "So did Lynn hit the numbers or what?" I asked her.

"No, and she was bummed," her sister told me.

"Oh, well. That's too bad."

"She was even more upset because she played those three numbers but they didn't come out. They *did* come out in the Play4, though!" she exclaimed.

"What? What are you saying? She was supposed to play the three numbers I gave her and add a fourth to do the Play4! Are you telling me she didn't do that?" I asked.

"Oh! I had no idea! She must have misunderstood! Wow, now she will *really* be bummed!"

Like I said before, we are only going to win if it is for our greater good. Unfortunately, I guess this was not something Lynn was supposed to have. But it did teach me a good lesson. It taught me that you really have to pay attention to what the message is and what you see. I thought I was pretty precise in the information I gave her, but somehow it got lost in translation. She did the Play3 instead of the Play4. Just that one little detail changed the entire outcome of the reading I had done. Imagine how many other times that happens: losing out on opportunities or even winnings because we don't take the information we psychically receive seriously or specifically enough. Unfortunately, I have not seen the winning numbers since then and I tell those who come looking to go with their own intuition. In this case it's just as good as mine, if not better!

And Speaking of Tickets...

Tapping into your clairvoyance definitely has multiple benefits. Sometimes, as with the lottery numbers, you'll receive very specific information from the other side. It was, without a doubt, exactly what you were supposed to see. Other times it's less specific. There is more room for translation in the message you are getting. Whichever way the communication is sent, the impressions still need to be interpreted. Frequently the messages come through while we are distracted. They can either be very subtle or more in-your-face, the stop-you-in-your-tracks-type messages. The psychic impression you get can be blinding or it may need clarification. Unless conducting a reading for someone, most of us tend to be more open to psychic visions when we are not trying as hard, especially when it's information for ourselves.

My client Laura told me of an experience she recently had where, luckily for her, she utilized her remote viewing unintentionally. She had been driving by herself, thinking of everything and nothing at all, singing to the radio. All of a sudden she had a clairvoyant premonition of a police car pulling someone over. She looked at her speedometer and realized she was going about twenty miles over the speed limit and immediately hit the brakes to slow down.

In less than half a mile, the car in front of her, which had not slowed at all, was pulled over. They were using radar and apparently pulling people over in that spot all day. Laura was very fortunate to have had her psychic insight when she did. As she drove by, very slowly, she saw there were multiple cars that had been pulled over. She knew she had made it through that speed trap, not by sheer luck, but by heeding her psychic remote vision. Her clairvoyant flash saved her the points on her license, the $215 fine, and the embarrassment of receiving a speeding ticket. Paying attention to the psychic vision she received as a premonition, or warning of something to come, made her day a much happier one.

Try It Now!

Psychic Radar

Okay, so maybe not right this second, but next time you go out and are the passenger in a car, notice if you have any psychic hits. Using your premonitory clairvoyance, notice if you see in your mind's eye a police car before you get to one. If so, were they using radar? Learning to trust your premonitions can help you avoid accidents as well. Allow those visions to come through clearly; it may make you a more conscious driver. And more importantly, may help keep you safe!

Complex or Simple

Connecting to your psychic vision can be as simple or as complex as you allow it to be. Knowing what clairvoyance is doesn't necessarily negate the complexities involved in how the connection works. In fact, the reality is, now that you are becoming more aware of what your psychic sight can show you, the diversity of how it will present and how it can be utilized makes it even more complicated. But think of it like a diamond: this multifaceted—and yes, complex—gift brings with it a brilliance equaled by no ordinary physical sense. Seeing with your clairvoyance helps you shine.

"My intuition comes up with better stuff than my head, I think."
~Ben Whishaw

Chapter Two
How Do I Know
I'm Using Clairvoyance?

What is the difference between imagination and clairvoyance? How do I know I'm not just remembering something and instead of remote viewing? Thirteenth-century poet and mystic Rumi said, "Close both eyes to see with the other." Learning to distinguish your psychic visions from anything else is simple once you understand what you are looking for.

Clairvoyance usually brings with it a feeling. This is because psychic sight is enhanced through the use of your other physical and psychic senses. (See chapter three.) Often, it is like an out-of-body sensation, like something isn't quite real or it feels mystical in some way. Sometimes this feeling is apprehension. When we are not sure what it is we are seeing, it can be confusing. And worse yet, if what we are seeing scares us in some way, we try really hard to get rid of the vision. This tends to shut down our psychic sight or causes us to believe it's only a figment of our imagination. Frequently, though, once we understand we are clairvoyantly seeing, we will experience some type of other sensation, like goose bumps. These physical sensations make our occurrence seem more substantial because they further validate our psychic gifts have kicked up.

Try It Now!

Remembering Goose Bumps

Think back to the last time you had goose bumps. If the goose bumps you had were because you were cold, disregard that instance and go to a time before that when they may have had more of a paranormal connection. Where were you? Do you remember the incident? Was it recent? Was it a long time ago? Do you remember how the goose bumps felt? Do you remember where you felt them on your body? Was it your arms? Was it your head? Was it your legs? Did you look at them? Did you actually physically see them?

How did you feel when you had the goose bumps? Were you shocked or surprised? Excited? Freaked out? Did it make you uncomfortable?

Write down anything you can remember. If you remember a time prior to that, go ahead and write that down as well. The main point of this exercise is to remember or determine how they made you feel. Writing the incidents down will help you explore those feelings.

Goose Bumps and Other Energetic Cues

Goose bumps are common enough, right? They pucker up your skin when you're cold and pop up when we're watching scary movies. They show up full force when you hear a beautiful song being sung with feeling, or when your child tells you he or she loves you and gives you the best sloppy, gooey, messy kiss ever. They can make you jump in your own skin when you are watching a scary movie or are creeped out. They alert you to danger as well, which is a form of psychic premonition or foresight, and they can even tell you when there is someone visiting from the other side. Goose bumps serve many purposes.

Now think about your imagination. Do goose bumps show up when you are imagining something? Do they make your hair stand on end because you are making something up? Not usually. They are reserved for what's real, or what you are experiencing as real. These little hair follicle soldiers are a very common indicator of a paranormal occurrence, and are one of the easiest ways to tell if you are dealing with a real showing of clairvoyance or just a bout of imagination.

Having said that, it doesn't mean that's the only time you are truly using your clairvoyance. Goose bumps need not always be present. This is merely a signal to let you know there is more going on than what your normal five senses are picking up. And this is only one way to determine if you are using your psychic abilities. You may also experience other physical sensations to let you know there is a flow or surge of metaphysical energy: your palms may get hot and tingly, your feet may feel like they are connected to the earth, your head may tickle, or your breath may even be taken away momentarily.

I was doing a reading for Trish last week. She was a new client and someone who'd never been to see any other psychic before. Admittedly she was very nervous. So, in order to calm her down and also connect with her energy, I did what I usually do in the beginning of a session. I explained how I worked and what normally happens during a reading with me.

I told Trish that before she even walked through the door, I had tuned in to her and connected to her energy during my five-minute meditation. Then I'd written down everything I clairvoyantly received while I waited for her to arrive. I continued by explaining how my head gets tingly during every session.

"No, I promise bugs will not jump out at you!" I told her. "My head just gets itchy and tingly when energy comes through in a reading. The metaphysical energy from the other side makes my hair stand up on my scalp, which is actually really good for the reading. It means there is energy I can connect to all around us. I also get goose bumps. Goose bumps are validation that what I'm getting is true and accurate, or that spirit is trying to come through with a message for you."

"Wow, okay," she replied. "But I'm still nervous and not sure about this."

"No worries. It will be relatively painless and calorie-free," I joked back.

So, for the first few minutes I began going over what I'd written down on the top of my sheet. What happened next amazed even me. I told her she'd just broken up with her boyfriend and that she was having dreams about them together. I also told Trish that her father was coming through along with her grandmother to give me this information, and to tell her she would definitely be going back to school to study nutrition. I went on to tell her that I thought she was experiencing her own intuitive moments; specifically, she had prophetic dreams (dreaming of what was to come in the future). She confirmed this, but that wasn't the amazing part. What made us both giggle like little girls was that we instantly experienced visible goose bumps up and down our bodies. She didn't need to validate what I said—we both knew it all to be true. After that, she was no longer afraid.

Try It Now!

Physical Indicator—Goosed by a Loved One

Bring your journal somewhere quiet where you can be alone and comfortable. You are going to put everything down and relax. Be ready to spend anywhere from ten to thirty minutes here, so be sure you're cozy!

Now, when you are ready, close your eyes and just feel the air around you. Feel the earth's energy as it comes up from the tips of your toes and moves through your feet into your ankles. Allow that energy to travel now up through your calves and your shins, and into your knees. Let it flow up through your shins and into your hips. As the energy moves, it clears out any negativity and brings positive energy to your joints, and your organs, and your spirit.

With every breath allow the beautiful energy to travel further up, through your abdomen, and your back, and your chest. As you take another deep breath any negativity still trapped in your trunk is exhaled, causing you to feel lighter and more relaxed. Let the energy continue to move up into your neck and your shoulders. Let it flow through your face and down your arms, through your hands and out the tips of your fingers. Finally let this energy move all the way up to the top of your head and allow it to flow out of your hair.

Now imagine a flower-lined pathway opening up in front of you. There is a gentle breeze blowing over your skin and you can feel the fine, soft hair on your arms as it slightly moves. As this path opens up more clearly, imagine seeing all of the colors around you.

Walking down the path coming toward you is one of your deceased loved ones. See them clearly: what colors they are wearing, their hair, and their eyes. As they come closer to you, imagine they are raising their arms toward you. You can feel their energy as they continue to come closer and closer toward you. Their features are clearer and you can now feel their breath on your face. As they whisper in your ear you feel them brush against you. Revel in this feeling for a few minutes. Then, allow them to pass through your body to continue their journey. You can feel their energy as it goes through you. Say goodbye to them.

Then, open your eyes. Do you have goose bumps? Did you feel them before you opened your eyes? Did you know you were getting goose bumps? When did you know? Before you saw your loved one? When you saw them? When they came closer? When they whispered to you? When they passed through you?

If you didn't get goose bumps, did you feel any type of sensation like a light breeze? Did you feel tingly or itchy? No worries—if you didn't experience goose bumps this time around you may need to try again, or try with a different loved one. Focus in and think of nothing else as you do the exercise. If you still didn't have any type of energy cue, it's okay! It just may not happen for you this way.

Seeing Spirals Again?

"I don't know if you understand this, but I keep seeing a spiral image. It's white and goes around and around," I told my client.

Audrey was having a phone reading. Unfortunately, because of that, I couldn't show her the drawing I kept scribbling on my paper. It was a spiral, similar to the one I drew in Jeanette's reading that indicated her father in New Zealand. This time, though, I knew it had nothing to do with that overseas country.

"I don't know what it is. Does it look like a shell, maybe? From the beach?" Audrey responded.

I'd just told her that I was getting a vacation on the water for her and she'd confirmed. I didn't think that was what I was seeing, though, and I told her as much.

"No, I don't think so. I do still see it, though. It's white and round, and I get the feeling it's very large," I insisted. "Usually if I continue to get an image that means it's significant in some way. I don't think they're going to give up until we get it!"

We both giggled a bit. I knew what I was saying to be true. I would keep receiving it until I was able to figure it out or until Audrey recognized it. So, laugh as we may, it wasn't going away.

"Hmmm. I really don't have any idea what it is. But can I ask you a question?"

"Sure, go for it!" I told her, knowing full well we would have to analyze that spiral some more.

"Okay. I would like to know about my relationship. Do you see it working out? Or should I move on? Or …"

She left it open for me to fill in the blanks. But this question just made the spiral image come in with more clarity.

"Do you know what the Guggenheim Museum is?" I heard the words and decided to share them, hoping it would at least describe what I was seeing, if not reference the actual thing I was seeing.

"Yes, I know what you're talking about."

"For some reason, when you ask about your boyfriend I'm seeing the Guggenheim, the spiral shape of the ramp system there. I also feel like this has something to do with your boyfriend situation. And I have to tell you, I'm not sure that it's positive. I'm seeing he's not around enough. There's a trust issue. Possibly due to all of the travel I see him doing. I don't know, but I feel like the spiral has something do with it. Do you know where the Guggenheim is located?" I continued.

"Yes, it's on the Upper East Side. I used to live near there," Audrey told me.

"Okay, well, that makes sense that you used to live there. But tell me what the Guggenheim has to do with your relationship? I'm getting more and more of a connection between the two. And it kind of feels sad or something."

"The only thing I can think of is the last date I went on with my boyfriend was when he took me to the Guggenheim. Could that be it?"

"Of course! That's it! I'm seeing the location of your last date along with your ex-boyfriend, and I call him 'ex' because I don't think you're still together. That's why this is so significant. Your loved ones are trying to let you know they see what you're going through and believe there's someone better out there for you. Like I said, there's a trust issue. You can't be sure of what he's doing. This makes it way too complicated, even though he's a nice guy and a smart guy. But obviously, they were showing me the Guggenheim for a reason and they weren't giving up until we got it!"

"Wow! I can't believe that. Everything you said makes perfect sense now," Audrey responded.

What I was seeing clairvoyantly for Audrey was logical to both of us, but only after I had put it all together using all of the clues I was receiving. I was repeatedly shown the spiral even though she hadn't immediately recognized it. Even after I brought up the Guggenheim, it still hadn't occurred to her what I was referring to. That's one of the ways I knew it was really my psychic sight and not just my imagination.

Seeing something over and over again, even with no additional evidence, can indicate that what you are receiving is a psychic vision. Generally, if it were just your imagination it wouldn't continue to show up. It also wouldn't tie into other psychic connections and fit with what you're tuning in to.

I am still always fascinated by how this works. It continues to surprise me when the visions I'm seeing tie pretty seamlessly into the other information I get, even though I don't always recognize it as such. This happens often when I describe my clairvoyant images, thinking I'm just using something as an example to explain what I'm seeing and then it turns out the example is actually what I'm supposed to bring up. For me it's an unexpected hit. For the client it's a "wow" moment—one of those bits of information that causes them to ask how I could possibly have known it. That's when you know for sure that it's absolutely, positively not your imagination.

Verifying Visions and Dragonflies

Verifying your clairvoyant visions isn't always immediately possible. Often you won't have validation until later, sometimes even much later. This is where belief, and yes, even faith comes in. You have to allow that there's more out there than what you may be able to touch or see with your physical eyes. Occasionally it may happen that you won't receive validation at all and you may always question if it's merely your imagination and not your clairvoyance responsible for the images you see.

For me, as a professional psychic, the same holds true. Quite regularly I have to trust that the visions I share with my clients are based on my clairvoyant abilities and not merely figments of my imagination. Sometimes this is made more difficult when the client is unable to recognize just what it is I'm talking about but desperately wants to. After all, they are looking for guidance and a lot of times are expecting you to give it to them with full directions. If you do A, then B will happen, and C will follow.

Along those lines, there's also the regular question of tuning in to their loved ones. There are two versions of this question: "Can you tell me who's here or if so-and-so is here?" and "How do I know if so-and-so is around me?" Again, there is the expectation that we will always be able to tell them "If you see A, then you will know B and C are with you."

This is very common, and believe me, I feel the same way when I'm a client! I want to know everything!

Wanda lost her husband a couple of years ago. He had an unexpected heart attack and it was devastating to her entire family. She asked me if it was meant to be that he had died. I told her, as I truly believe, that there are multiple exit points in our lives and this was one of his. I also explained that though she doubted it, he did love her. And he most definitely loved his kids. He needed them all to know that, because he hadn't had the opportunity to tell them before he died.

"But, how do I know? And how do I know he's around? I'm just not sure what is happening. I'm not sure what to do or how to trust that he's there. I kind of feel like he's come to me, but I can't tell," she told me, and it was obvious she was distressed.

"It is very difficult to know whether it's really them when we think they are around us. I totally understand what you mean," I responded.

"Okay, I just wasn't sure if he is still there or not," she said.

"Good luck with everything, and again, I'm so sorry for all of you. Oh, wait. Dragonflies? Do dragonflies mean anything to you?" I asked her. "I was just interrupted as I was talking and I saw an image of a dragonfly. Do you know why? Does this have to do with your husband?"

"Oh, I have absolutely no idea," she replied as she pondered the possibilities.

"All right. Just know that he's around you when you see the dragonfly. And he's there to help you," I told her.

Neither one of us had any idea what that was supposed to mean. After all, dragonflies are prevalent during the summer. They will even land on your hand if you hold it still enough. Telling her to look for the dragonflies was a huge generalization. I never thought it would amount to much, and I actually thought maybe I told her that because she was so desperate for a sign and dragonflies are very common psychic signs. That is, until a few weeks later.

Her daughter, Brianna, is friends with my daughter, Molly. She was over and we were talking about their upcoming move. They'd decided they were going to change residences to have a new start in a fresh town in a new home. They had been looking during the few weeks that had passed and found what they believed was the perfect house.

"That's great, Bri! I'm so happy for you guys!" I told her as her mom pulled up.

"Hi, Wanda," I greeted her when she got out of her car.

"Wow, Melanie. You're not going to believe this. Did Brianna tell you we found our new house?"

"Yes? Why is that unbelievable?" I asked her.

"That's not the unbelievable part. What's unbelievable is the dragonfly!"

"Wait, what are you talking about?"

"We looked at a lot of houses. Then the realtor brought us to this one. It hadn't been shown for about a week and it was all closed up. Well, when we walked in there was a huge dragonfly just sitting there watching us. At first I thought maybe that was Paul's sign, but I wasn't sure. Then it followed us from room to room and just landed and stared at us each time. That's how I knew for sure it was him. He was telling us to buy the house!" Wanda told me.

"Oh! That's fantastic! I'm so happy for you! Now I know for sure that it wasn't my imagination!"

What makes this story even more incredible is months later I asked their permission to write about it in this book, and they wholeheartedly agreed. Brianna told me, "Oh my God! I'm doing a speech in my public speaking class tomorrow about what dragonflies mean to me now!" Talk about validation! It's as if Paul was giving his seal of approval on my book as well. Thanks, Paul!

Sometimes patience is all you need to recognize clairvoyance over imagination. As a working psychic, I'm constantly tasked to share my psychic sight with my clients as well as my friends. I have to believe that what I'm telling them is more than merely my imagination. After all, it's not my life we're talking about; it's theirs. I need to trust that what I tell them will be relevant to them.

Try It Now!

Psychic Vision or Imagination?

Think about the last time you questioned whether you were having a clairvoyant, psychic, or intuitive moment. Did you trust it? Did you believe what you were seeing was real? Or did you assume it was your imagination? If you thought it was your imagination, why did you think that? Was it because you don't trust your psychic vision? Or do you not believe you are able to have psychic sight? Is there another reason? Do you just doubt your own personal abilities? Was it not clear enough? Was it something other than what you expected?

How often do you find yourself questioning whether what you're seeing is psychic viewing or just a figment of your imagination? Start writing these situations down so you have a record of them. You may find there is a pattern!

There really is no perfect way to guarantee you're using your clairvoyance and not your imagination. Psychic vision is not like math or spelling. It's a gift that you need to believe in to bring out more. However, there is a way to increase your propensity for knowing whether it's truly your intuition you are using: practice. Practice may not make perfect, but the more you work on developing your psychic gifts, the easier it will be to determine they're really there. When you utilize your intuitive abilities you become a better person and closer to who you are meant to be; you are practicing what your spirit already knows. Melissa Alvarez, professional psychic and author, says in her latest book, "You have been given your gifts for a reason; use them to enhance and embrace your true soul essence as you make your way on the earthly plane" (Alvarez, 2013). You are living in a human body, but your spirit is what energizes you. Use that energy and enjoy your psychic birthright!

"Psychic senses are the coolest thing since sliced bread. Scratch that.
Psychic senses were cool way before sliced bread!"
—from *Psychic Abilities for Beginners*

Chapter Three
Friends of the Third Eye: Clairvoyance and the Other Clairs

By now you've either fully embraced your clairvoyant abilities and excelled, or you've at least had some success with the exercises you've done. It's possible you've done them repeatedly, which is my hope. However, some of you may be feeling as though you're missing something or you're not quite receiving psychic images. This can happen even if you are still able to tune in. Don't fret! Everyone is different and everyone develops in their own way. Seeing images to help you identify your extrasensory clues is what you're doing when you tap into your clairvoyance, but there's so much more to psychic ability! Extrasensory perception, or ESP, is not just about psychic sight; otherwise, ESP would just be clairvoyance. It's so much more.

Clairvoyance is sometimes used interchangeably with the words *psychic* or *intuition*. The reason for this is simple. Clairvoyance is most often a prevalent psychic sense and the one used most for remote viewing. However, clairvoyance is simply clear vision. There are so many more psychic senses to take advantage of!

Meet the Clairs

Many people believe if you're not born with it, you can't develop it, but I disagree. I know being a natural clairvoyant or psychic usually yields better and more detailed information when tuning in to your psychic messages. However, I also know that you can absolutely study how to tap into the other side and communicate with learned abilities. I've sat with students as their peer and I've taught students as their teacher. It's amazing being present with others who have never connected with their clairvoyance before and seeing their excitement when they are able to make that link. And they *do* connect. This chapter will open you up to developing your gifts more then ever before.

Clairvoyance is enhanced when utilizing all of your senses. This includes your other *clairs*, or "clear psychic abilities." The most common are *clairaudience* ("hearing"), *clairsentience* ("feeling"), and *claircognizance* ("knowing"). There's also *clairempathy* ("emotion"), *clairgustance* ("tasting"), *clairalience*, *clairolfaction*, *clairescence* ("scent"), and *clairtangency* ("touch").

Combined with your clairvoyance, these senses can give you a better overall understanding of the psychic messages you are receiving. For example, if you are psychically viewing Little Italy, a location in New York City known for its Italian restaurants, what better way then to enhance your clairvoyant images than with clairgustance or clairalience. To see an image of somewhere in Little Italy, even if it's a known restaurant, may not give you a full view of the area. You may think it's any restaurant, anywhere. But seeing an image of New York City, and smelling delicious Italian food, and tasting sauce the way your grandma made it will help really key you in to where you might be.

Or imagine clairvoyantly seeing someone's near future and viewing them hooked up to all kinds of monitors and tubes in a hospital bed. Scary, right? An immediate translation may indicate doom and gloom. That would be very difficult. This can be confusing if you don't understand it. Your brain may immediately take you to a place that's entirely different than the actual situation. But if along with your remote viewing you also feel warm and cozy and you smell the unmistakable fresh scent of a new baby, your whole perspective changes, and it becomes not about death, but about birth.

How Do I See?

Following the signals you receive is easier when you allow for all of your senses to be utilized. The images you see with your clairvoyance may not always be identifiable without additional clues. The information becomes more ascertainable, and though there are no guarantees, you will definitely have a more accurate picture. Just think about your regular senses. Eating is enhanced through smell, and sight is improved through sound. The same holds true for your psychic senses.

Try It Now!

Identifying Your Senses

Below is a list of activities or things. Write them in your journal or on a blank piece of paper in a column down the left side of the page. Then, create additional columns headed *Primary, Secondary,* and *More* (or you can simply fill in the blanks below). For each item write the primary sense (taste, touch, smell, sight, or hearing) used when performing the activity, and then list the secondary. You may find that using more senses will increase your enjoyment or understanding of what it is you are doing!

Activity/Object	*Primary*	*Secondary*	*More*
Acting			
Animals			
Baking			
Children			
Christmas			
Concert			
Date			
Flying			

Activity/Object	Primary	Secondary	More
Football			
Gum Drops			
Hawaii			
Hospital			
July 4th			
Loving			
Mall			
Party			
Playground			
Police			
Pool			
Reading			
Running			
School			
Shopping			
Telephone			
Television			
Working			
Workshop			

Were you able to assign each one? Did it make sense? Did it feel like a lightbulb went off while you were doing it? Were you surprised by the senses you actually use for each activity? Which sense was most prevalent? Were some more difficult than others? Did you feel more able of recognizing certain senses than others?

After you've answered everything, go back and write down the clair sense that each represents. For example, if you put down "sight" for one, clairvoyance would be the corresponding psychic sense.

Now that you know what the clair senses are, we can focus in on each one individually. When you don't have any restraints placed on you as to which sense you are allowed to use, everything becomes clearer without even having to think about it. The process just happens, almost as if you were pre-programmed like a robot, though of course you still have freedom of choice.

Clairaudience—Did You Hear That?

Clairaudience, or clear hearing, is the psychic ability to hear sounds without using your physical hearing. Generally, regardless of how intuitively developed you are, you won't hear sentences as complete or as detailed as you do with your physical ears. However, the more you tune in and practice, the clearer the sounds will be.

A while back I was doing a reading for Courtney over the phone. We had talked about many different topics during her hour-long session, from when she would be moving to where she would work. We'd discussed just about everything. I told her I was receiving the information through my clairvoyance. I saw a map to show me where she would live. I saw a hospital which allowed me to tell her that yes, indeed, I could tell going back to school to become a nurse was in the cards for her. Every question had been answered.

Then she asked, "Where is the information coming from? I mean, I know you're connected to the other side, but who is showing you all of this?"

"I get information from my loved ones, my guides, and angels as well as your loved ones, guides, and angels. Essentially, I tell everyone it's your energy the universe shares with me. I really don't have much influence over it. I just ask for anyone to come through who is positive and relevant to you and your life," I answered.

"Oh, I thought it might have been someone specific. I was hoping to hear from someone I lost last year," she continued, and though I couldn't see her, I could detect tears were beginning to gently flow.

"Hmmm. Well, I see dark hair, on the shorter side. I see a big, giant smile."

"Okay, that could be him. I'm not sure, though. Do you get a name?"

Now, usually when I connect to the other side, I'm able to get initials of the people who are trying to come through. Occasionally I will get full names, or both first and last initials. But Courtney's loved one was not helping me out. I wasn't getting any initials or names.

"I don't know. I'm not really getting anything. Though I'm hearing Michael Jackson singing. Do you like Michael Jackson? Did he? I'm sorry I'm not getting his name."

Luckily for me, she did not suffer with psychic amnesia. She immediately made the connection he was trying to get me to make by the clue he sent me from the other side.

"His name was Michael. And his middle name was Jack. That makes perfect sense. Thank you so much for letting me know he's around. You have no idea what that means to me!"

Courtney's story is pretty common. By using more than one psychic sense I was able to tune in to her friend, whom she missed very much. I gave her evidence that it was him by providing her with a name I heard with my clairaudience rather than perceived with my clairvoyance. So much more evidence can be gathered by using multiple abilities.

There are no set rules about who will or won't be clairaudient. Anyone can be naturally gifted with this psychic sense. However, those who have special talents physically will tend to be drawn to the same type of ability on the metaphysical spectrum. This occurs organically, because they are already tuned in to that physical sense and accustomed to using it. Therefore, the information garnered by using those senses is more recognizable.

Musicians, for instance, have more of a propensity for clairaudience. Because they are so trained in key and pitch, they have a better ear for sound. This holds true when trying to understand words or various sounds coming from the other side. Think of a lion's roar. Can you imagine it clearly? Does it sound right to you? Does it sound full? If so, great! If not, why? Do you need to actually hear it to be able to discern it? Recognizing sound is the basis for clairaudience.

What makes clairaudience more interesting is that there are a variety of sounds to represent different things. Think of a horn. There are a multitude of horns out there and every one of them is unique. Older Jeeps, for instance, sound like they have a toy horn, whereas a Volvo will just about wake the dead. A Dodge pickup is just as loud, but it has a completely different sound than a Mustang.

Birds chirp, but never the same way between breeds. Dogs bark, children laugh, and telephones ring. Each has a unique tone or sound or vibrato. The vibration is different as well. Now, imagine the messengers from the other side trying to send you a horn beep. It's a pretty generic sound, isn't it? That doesn't mean you'll know exactly which vehicle it may belong to; instead, it leaves plenty of room for interpretation. That's exactly what our helpers from the other side will do—send us information that, although maybe a personal reference for us, is also universally recognizable.

The Dalai Lama said, "When you talk, you are only repeating what you know; but when you listen, you may learn something new." He's on to something. By truly listening to what's around you and what others say, you not only hear the sounds, but you can also pick up the subtleties. There are always ways to say things that can alter their meanings. Saying "oh, sure!" when asked if you'd like a piece of chocolate cake versus "oh, sure" when asked to scrub the toilet will produce an entirely different connotation. Listening is key to tuning in.

Try It Now!

Listen Up—Practicing Clairaudience

Once again, go somewhere you won't be disturbed and can be comfortable. If you can, put on some soft, lyric-free background music. Sit or lie down, closing your eyes.

Now inhale, allowing the breath to flow through your body, supplying you with life-affirming air. Inhale again, letting the oxygen into your organs and your blood. With every inhalation, imagine slowing your heartbeat to a comfortable rhythm. And with every exhalation, imagine all the energy you no longer need leaving your body, clearing you and leaving you refreshed.

Continue breathing, keeping your eyes closed, and begin focusing on a little tiny dot of light inside your mind. Imagine it in front of your eyes. Allow that dot to grow larger, brighter in front of you. As it expands, let it grow even bigger, so large in fact that it extends all the way around you, keeping you safe and secure.

Soak that in for a bit, breathing in and out, allowing your bubble of protection to continue growing. Now, imagine feeling the sun shining down on you, warming you from the inside out, and the perfect temperature. As you inhale, imagine being on a beautiful, tropical island complete with white sands and turquoise waters. You are alone, but not lonely, perfectly content and comfortable lying on the sand.

Now, listen as the waves gently lap up against the shoreline. You can also hear a soft breeze as it blows through the palm trees, blowing away any further negativity that may be attached to you. Hear the call of the seagulls, almost as though they are talking directly to you. Take it all in as you breathe deeply.

Next, imagine while you remain lying on the sand with the water nearby that you can hear someone coming toward you. It is your spirit guide, your own personal helper from the other side, who is coming to give you a message. They've taken on a human form, regardless of how they may normally appear, so you will able to relate to them more easily. As they get closer, you can hear the swoosh of the sand as they displace it with their bare feet.

You can hear the movement of the fabric on their body as they walk toward you. They are so close their breath meshes with your breath, in and out, gently inhaling and exhaling. You can now hear their breath immediately next to your ear. And they tell you to listen. They have something important to share with you. Possibly about your next direction in life, or maybe a hello from a deceased loved one, or special congratulations for something coming up or recently passed in your life. They may have an answer to a specific question you've been requesting guidance on.

Listen. Just listen. Do nothing else. Don't ask any questions. Pay attention to nothing else. When you've received your message, go ahead and take another deep breath. Then, open your eyes.

What did your guide tell you? Could you hear it? Was it clear? Did it make sense? Was it something you expected? Was it an answer to a question? Was it a new direction? Did it refer to a specific situation in your life? Was it about your next step? Did it relate to a family member or friend?

Clairsentience—Can You Feel It?

Clairsentience is one of the most common senses. Right up there with clairvoyance, it ranks on the top of the list for psychic senses we use most often. However, it is not always recognized. This is a tough ability to distinguish, mostly because it's hard to prove. This is your gut instinct, your intuitive hunch. This is when you feel things psychically.

One of the preliminary ways I receive information is through clairsentience. Feeling whether something is off is a huge part of how I do readings. That feeling is usually clarified through the use of my other psychic senses, such as clairvoyance. That first initial gut reaction guides my psychic vision.

This occurred during a reading with Lisa, who came to me because she needed guidance. She was in a difficult situation and needed some help, as is the case with many of my clients. So, a couple of minutes into the reading, she began asking me questions when I told her I saw divorce in her near future.

"Okay, but when do you see him actually moving out?" she asked, clearly aware of the upcoming separation.

Now, I knew she was hoping to hear he'd be gone right away. But my gut had dropped into a hollow inside. This told me it wasn't to be. Then, I saw pumpkins.

"I don't think that's going to happen for a while," I responded. "I'm getting October. I know that's about four months away, but I don't believe it's going to happen any sooner than that."

"Oh, that stinks. Are you sure?" She laughed, trying to make light of it, but she was absolutely serious.

"Yup, sorry!"

"That's fine. I actually didn't expect it to happen right away, I was just hoping. What about my house? I'm putting it on the market for sale by owner. I want to sell it right away."

Again my stomach felt like it dropped away, and I knew it would be a very hard sell. It wasn't going anywhere for quite a while. I felt like her energy was way too attached to the house to let it go. But I also felt like everything would work out with it.

"I don't believe you will sell your home anytime soon. It will take a very long time, if it sells at all. But maybe down the road you will be moving at some point."

"Wow. Thanks. You're just full of happy news!" she replied.

I felt bad and tried to soften the blows, but short of lying to her, there was nothing else I could do. I knew she was hoping for different answers but sometimes there are just none to be had.

Lisa came back to see me a couple months later. She wanted to know if everything was still on track or if things would be changing from what I originally told her. Before she came in the second time, I did my normal channeling and wrote down whatever information I received. Now, again what's interesting is that I'd scribbled and doodled "December" as being very significant, but I wasn't sure why until later. I never remember what I tell people in readings and this was no different. But I knew that everything that needed to be said would be.

"So, what do you see now? Do you see anything different from last time?" she asked as soon as she sat down.

"Well, I don't remember what I told you last time. But I do feel like there's a divorce and your ex will be moving out of your house," I responded.

"That's right. Can you tell me when? You told me something when I was here before, but I just want to know what you feel now."

Now, what's funny is that she remembered and had even typed up her notes from her last reading. And she knew I'd told her I saw October as the time frame for her ex-husband to be leaving.

"I think something's shifted and it's happening now in December. I feel like it was supposed to be the fall, probably October, but something changed with court or something, so expect it to be more around Christmas versus Halloween."

"Wow. Okay. That's kind of why I came back! I did just have something with the lawyers, and the date for the divorce and him moving out is now December. It was supposed to be October. All right, I trust you! As long as this is it!"

"No worries, it will happen around that time," I confirmed.

Lisa was able to acknowledge the changes that had occurred within her divorce case. This helped me to validate the feelings I was getting. My clairsentient vibe helped me to address what she needed to know. I felt heavy and empty, so I knew it was not necessarily what she was hoping to hear, but it was her reality. Turns out, my clairsentience was correct. If I hadn't gone with my gut feelings during either of the readings, they wouldn't have been as accurate. If I'd ignored them, it would have just set my client up for failure, as she wouldn't have been expecting things to take so long.

Try It Now!

Go with Your Gut

For this exercise you're going to tap into your gut instincts. You need to learn to trust what your clairsentience tells you. For each of the objects/situations listed below, you will tune in to how you feel toward it and check off either Positive or Negative. By accessing how each makes you feel, you are becoming more aware of how your clairsentience will present itself. Along the way you just may learn a thing or two about yourself and your own life. Be sure to allow enough time to give yourself the chance to receive your answers. When you are done, go back and look over what you've recorded.

	Positive	Negative
Yourself as a whole	❏	❏
Your home	❏	❏
Your job	❏	❏
Your significant other	❏	❏
Your family	❏	❏
Your best friend	❏	❏
Your last vacation	❏	❏
Your recreation	❏	❏
Your health	❏	❏
Your physical appearance	❏	❏
Your personality	❏	❏
Your confidence	❏	❏
Your education	❏	❏
Your finances	❏	❏

Go back and review your entries. Are there some you are surprised with? Do they all make sense? Do you have more positive or negative entries? Were they all positive? Were they all negative? Do you think this exercise will help you make changes in your life to make it better? Why or why not? Were you able to feel how the positive and negative responses presented in your body, mind, and spirit?

Claircognizance—What Do You Know?

Claircognizance is not always easy to recognize. Knowing something just because you know it can be a hard concept to grasp. And seldom does it happen that you even realize you are experiencing claircognizance until afterward. The "that's what I thought!" or "I knew that was going to happen!" kind of moments are products of clear knowing. These episodes usually prove themselves after the fact, and we are usually the only ones who will know we had those moments of psychic clarity.

My daughter was out with her friends the other day. All of a sudden I knew I had to call her. I was absolutely sure something was wrong, but I couldn't put my finger on exactly what it was. So I called her—no answer. I texted her—no answer. Now, if you have a teenager with a cell phone, you can feel my pain. It's rare that they have their phone volume turned on, and even rarer that they notice you are trying to get in touch with them. But this was different. I knew there was more going on, so I kept calling and texting—to no avail.

Molly, my daughter, was with her friend Morgan and a few others. So I decided to try Morgan's phone. Luckily, after almost half an hour, I was able to reach them. Before she could even tell me anything, I asked what was wrong and if the police were there, because I psychically saw flashing lights in my mind.

"Yes, but it's all going to be okay. They're pulling in now. The grounds-keeper says we're trespassing and he closed the gates on our vehicles." Apparently they had gone into the town park reserves, which had a strict close-at-dusk policy. They stayed in the park too long and the crotchety property manager, who obviously had dealt with punks before, decided to detain them by locking the gate and calling the police.

"Why isn't Molly answering the phone?" I asked Morgan.

"Her phone was in the Jeep and she didn't want to call you until after the police came and she knew more of what was happening," she answered.

"Fine, keep me on the line while you talk to them!"

I could hear the police talking with them.

"No worries. I'm not sure why he panicked like that. Just do me a favor and don't come to the park after dark," said the cop.

I could hear Molly trying to start her Jeep.

"Why isn't it starting? Did you break down?" the police officer asked.

"No—I just need to rebuild my carburetor," Molly answered with a chuckle. "It just takes a minute to catch."

Then I heard the Jeep start, and I have to admit, rather than being mad, I too found myself chuckling a bit. She was having a conversation with the police about her mechanical issues. They obviously were not going to arrest them. The relief was overwhelming.

Later, when she asked how I knew something was wrong, I couldn't tell her anything other than I just knew. "When something feels off, it is" (Hicks, 2011). Claircognizance is that sense of knowing things without knowing why you know them. There usually is no tangible reason for being aware of something other than psychic ability.

Try It Now!

What Do You Know?

How claircognizant are you? Check which answer applies to each of the following situations to find out.

Know:	Never	Sometimes	Often	Always
Phone will ring	❏	❏	❏	❏
Who's calling	❏	❏	❏	❏
You'll run into someone	❏	❏	❏	❏
Something is off	❏	❏	❏	❏
Something good's coming	❏	❏	❏	❏
Someone's pregnant	❏	❏	❏	❏
Partner's lying	❏	❏	❏	❏
Someone's coming	❏	❏	❏	❏
Someone's sick	❏	❏	❏	❏
Someone passed	❏	❏	❏	❏
Going to be good day	❏	❏	❏	❏
Going to be bad day	❏	❏	❏	❏
Partner has good surprise	❏	❏	❏	❏

Money's coming	❏	❏	❏	❏
Unexpected bill is coming	❏	❏	❏	❏

Now add your own!

_____	❏	❏	❏	❏
_____	❏	❏	❏	❏
_____	❏	❏	❏	❏
_____	❏	❏	❏	❏

How did you do? If you answered Always to all of them, you are extremely claircognizant! This may be your most prevalent sense! If you answered Often to most of them, you are a clair-cognizant person! This sense is used regularly for you. If you answered Sometimes most often, you are open to this psychic knowing sense but should believe in your instincts more. If you answered Never to most of the situations, chances are you don't use your claircognizant abilities. This may be because you don't recognize them or it may be that this is not one of your stronger senses.

Remember, however, that you are doing this exercise from memory. Keep this list by you and note each time you have pre-cognizant knowledge of any of these situations, meaning you know they are going to happen before they do. You may notice now that you are aware of the possibility, you will start using your claircognizant gifts more often!

Regardless of how this exercise went for you, don't discount any knowing experiences you have. Any time you just know something, think of it as a gift from the universe!

Clairempathy—I Feel You!

Clairempathy is very similar to, and can even be called, clairsentience. It's about feeling something on a more emotional level. Just as we say we have empathy for someone, meaning we feel what they are going through, when we use our clairempathy we can connect to them on a psychic level in the same way.

Clairempathy is also the psychic gift we use when we walk into a room and we can feel the energy of the people in it without even talking to them. It's the vibe we get when we share someone else's emotion, like when we get excited simply because they are. Children tend to be very psychic and empathic, so much so that when I work with them I often have them rewind themselves to get back into their own bodies. I literally have them spin around backward. It tends to reprogram them and break their clairempathic bond, allowing them to be themselves again. Afterward, they can tell the difference. It's one of the methods I use to teach them about their clairempathic powers, and it's just plain cool.

People often ask me if I've always been psychic. I tell them yes and no. When I was younger, I was always able to read people. I could just kind of tell who they were. I could also tell if I liked them or not and if there was something wrong with them, either emotionally or physically. It made me feel like I had an interesting perspective and that I was a good judge of character. However, back then I had no idea that I was actually tuning in to people using my clairempathy. Now, though I still do it, I like to give people a second chance. I realize the energy I pick up on may just be because they've had a rough day or they were just yelled at by someone. When you pick up on energy, it can be difficult to move past the initial blast.

My husband uses his clairempathy regularly with his customers. It's his way of gauging whether people are going to be honest with him or whether they will try to rip him off in some way. So far, he's been right on the money, literally!

I have a client, Mallory, who comes in to see me a few times each year. She generally comes in for readings, but occasionally she needs a little healing done as well.

"I like what I do. But every day by the end of my shift, I'm utterly exhausted. I don't understand it. I go to work happy, but when I leave I always feel miserable. I don't know what's going on. Do I have something wrong with me physically? Do you think I have lupus or MS or something? What about lyme? It just doesn't make sense."

Now, this particular client has had many readings about her relationships, her finances, her family, and other miscellaneous details. I've also told her many times that she's very intuitive.

"All right, let me tune in and see what's happening," I told Mallory.

I tuned in to her body and did a scan using my clairempathy as well as my clairvoyance. I felt for any pockets of illness or disease. When I felt a couple spots that were off, I used my clairvoyance to see if they were solid black, indicating actual disease, or just filmy or cloudy dark spots, which tells me they are just areas of discomfort. Luckily, there were no solid spots and I didn't feel anything else that was off with her physically, so I told her.

"I don't think there's anything wrong with you, though, as you know, I'm not a medical professional. Let me tune in to your day and what's happening at work," I explained.

Normally I would just tap into her energy and pick up what was going on. But because she specifically asked about disease, I wanted to be sure to rule anything of that ilk out. I didn't want to overlook something that could be problematic or even dangerous for her even though I hadn't originally picked it up. So now I focused on her daily grind.

"Got it. I know what's happening. And I know how to fix it!" I told her excitedly.

"Really? Are you sure I'm not sick? It's just so strange that I go in to work and by the end of the day I'm completely wiped out, in every way," she said again.

"Nope, you're not sick at all. But all of the patients who come in to see you are!" I told her.

Mallory worked in a doctor's office. She mainly dealt with the sick patient appointments and did the basics for them when they came in. She took their blood pressures, weighed them in, and more importantly, asked what was bothering them.

"You see, when you ask them what's wrong, they complain. They tell you, and rightly so, everything that's happening with them, causing them to suffer. They explain in full detail how bad they feel, and as they do, you take it all in. Not only are you taking on their emotional state, but you are also feeling their illness. It's no wonder you're crashing by the time you go home!"

"You know what? I think you're absolutely right! That makes perfect sense! I can't believe I didn't think about that. Thank you so much, but now what do I do?"

So I then taught her how to protect herself.

Try It Now!

Protect Yourself

If you haven't already learned how to properly protect yourself from taking on others' emotions or illnesses, it's time to start! This protection exercise can be done anywhere once you know how to do it. For now, you need to be comfortable and relaxed and in a place where you won't be disturbed.

Close your eyes and breathe until you feel totally at ease and ready to continue. Imagine you have in your hands a lightweight fabric. This fabric has the same properties as a regular glass mirror but is much more manageable. Now, extend this mirror fabric out in front of you with the reflective properties aimed away from your body. As you do, notice you can still see clearly through the material.

Spread that material out, allowing it to hang all around you completely: below your feet, next to you in a complete circle, above your head, and forming a bubble shape. You can still see beyond the mirror and breathe through the fabric easily, deeply, clearly.

Then, allow the mirror to expand even further, and as it does it grows in strength as well. Any energy that comes toward you or at you that is unwanted, unnecessary, or negative will now be reflected back at the person or people that are sending out these vibrations. This protective mirror fabric easily keeps out energy that may otherwise have been absorbed by your clairempathic gifts, allowing you to be free from anything that will cause you discomfort in any way.

Any time you feel like there is any negative energy directed toward or just bouncing around you, surround yourself with the mirror fabric to protect you entirely. Enjoy the feeling as it warms you and keeps you safe and secure. Revel in the fact that you no longer have to take on others' energy in order to read them, but instead can just understand them from a distance.

When you are ready, open your eyes. Could you feel the fabric? Did you feel the mirror reflecting back others' energy? Do you feel lighter, less burdened, or unencumbered by energy that doesn't belong to you? Were you able to visualize the mirror fabric? Did you feel it in your hands? Luckily for you, this exercise can be utilized any time you need to if ever you feel overwhelmed in any way.

Clairgustance and Clairalience— Taste It, Smell It

The clairs are not just friends of clairvoyance, but also work hand in hand with each other. The most common combinations of physical senses work the same way as psychic senses. Smelling and tasting kind of go hand in hand. They enhance each other. Imagine opening a jar of pickles. You can easily smell them and taste them even if you're not actually placing one in your mouth.

One of the ways I can tell my mom is around, from the other side, is through my clairgustance and clairalience. It doesn't matter where I am or what I'm doing, I can always tell it's her. She used to make chili, but it wasn't normal spicy chili. It had a very distinct flavor that I loved. Every once in a while I smell it, though no one is cooking it. Once I smell it, I know it's inevitable that I will taste it. Interestingly enough, it often happens when I'm vacuuming, which is funny because she hated to clean! I love when she says hi to me that way.

A few years ago I was doing a reading for Warren in my office. We had gone over most everything on his list of questions. I'd told him, and he verified, that he would be moving within a few months for a new job. I also told him he would enjoy his job, but they would challenge him in the beginning to see if he could handle it. He thanked me for the warning. Then I told him I was seeing some kind of garden from his youth. He confirmed they'd had a family garden growing up.

"Oh well. I was hoping to hear from my sister. I guess she doesn't have anything to say today," Warren said. He'd been in before. His sister had come through with messages of love and a basic hello to let him know she was around and still part of his life.

"I'm sorry, Warren. I'm not sure why she's not showing up," I told him.

"That's okay. I know she's still around. I guess I was just looking for some evidence that she's really there. I know last time she gave you something specific. I was hoping for that again."

As he was talking, I began to have an overwhelming craving for the strangest thing.

"I wish I had something for you," I said, wondering why I wasn't getting anything. My craving was growing. I was smelling pumpkins and tasting ice cream. My mind started to wander and I was wondering whether I should take the kids to the farm after work, where they had a fresh ice cream shack. I started to doubt whether I was too distracted to connect for Warren. I was getting confused. I wasn't even seeing the ice cream place the right way; it was more like a small pumpkin patch.

"It's all right. I understand. Maybe next time," he said.

"Look, I have to be honest. I feel like I'm kind of ripping you off. All of a sudden I'm totally distracted. I'm debating whether to take my kids out for ice cream after we're done here! My apologies! I can't help tasting ice cream, though—pumpkin, my favorite. I love the way the farm near my house makes it from scratch. I can smell the farm already!" I admitted.

"Oh. My. God. She did it! Jennifer came through! Thank you so much!" he exclaimed, tears forming in his eyes.

"Wait, what do you mean? I'm not understanding."

"When we were young, we had a garden, like you said earlier. One year we had an overabundance of pumpkins come in. We made pumpkin bread, pumpkin pie, pumpkin cookies! You name it, we made it. We even carved a whole bunch of them for Halloween. Then we decided to try and make pumpkin ice cream. It probably would have been better if we had managed to take all of the seeds out! That was the worst pumpkin ice cream we'd ever tasted!" he shared.

"I'm so glad! That's awesome!"

"Thank you so much!" he said, gratitude written all over his tear-streaked face.

Although I didn't recognize it for what it was, I was very grateful that Warren was able to. It obviously meant the world to him to hear from his sister. What's even better is that she came through with something that was an incredibly funny and special memory they both shared. She sent me the pumpkin ice cream in such a way I was able to smell it, taste it, and see it.

Sometimes smell is more prevalent, but it can also be combined with taste, even if it's not something you'd readily think of. Take, for instance, cigarettes or cigars. Most of us can readily identify the scent of cigarette smoke, whether we've ever smoked ourselves or not. After the smell comes the taste. If you've smoked, you have firsthand knowledge of what it tastes like. If you never have, you may just taste what the exhaled smoke tastes like based on your own personal exposure. This also happens with perfume. If you've ever sprayed cologne in your mouth, unintentionally, you know it has a very distinct, strong taste. Anything you can smell, you can also taste. The same holds true for your psychic senses.

Try It Now!

Did You Taste That Smell?

This exercise is designed to connect you to your loved ones on the other side. If you're not quite there with your connections, just imagine you are and run with whatever feels right.

Focus on one loved one who's passed. Take a nice deep breath. Now, if you had to assign a scent or a flavor to them, what would it be? Would it be food? Perfume? Smoke? Flowers? Outdoors? Ocean?

Once you've decided on what best represents them, bring it to the next level by trying to actually smell and taste what you have related to them. Can you do it? Is it strong? Is your clairgustance or clairalience stronger? Which was easier?

After you've finished the first one, move on to another deceased loved one. You may find it's simpler to do one particular person over another, especially if they were known for something like cooking or smoking. Was this second one easier to do? Harder? The same? Do you think it made a difference that you've already done it? Does it feel more comfortable?

When you are done connecting to your deceased loved ones, try it with someone who is still alive. Do it with a few people. Is it easier if they are still here? Or easier to do if they've passed?

Clairtangency—Touch This!

Hands-on healing is healing through touch or feel. This works because of energy. We all have energy that flows through us and around us and is generally what we tap into when we use our psychic abilities. When I do Reiki, a form of energy healing that helps adjust your *chi*, or life force energy, I usually use my clairtangent gifts to read my client's body to determine if they have any aches or discomforts or energetic blocks that need to be cleared. Though everyone has energy, each person's energy is individual and very unique.

It is this energy that we tune in to when we use clairtangency. One of the most prominent forms of psychic touch is *psychometry*. This is simply based on the premise that all objects, not just people, hold energy and that energy can be tapped into when we touch the object. By tuning in to the object we are able to garner a variety of information about it, sometimes including who owns it, where they got it, what's happening in their lives, and more.

I teach this form of clairtangency in my intuitive development classes. Much to the amazement of the students, it has a very high success rate. Psychic touch is sort of a gateway into the other psychic senses, specifically clairvoyance.

Vicky learned this firsthand during one of my workshops.

"I don't think I can do this. I've never done it before. I really just came to the class to get a reading from you. I didn't realize I was going to have to do work," she said when asked to participate in her first psychic exercise.

"Haaa! You're too funny! Well, now you know. You get to tune in to your own intuition. And you get to have fun doing it!" I told her.

"All right, I suppose I can try. But I have absolutely no psychic ability whatsoever, so I make no promises," she said nervously.

"No worries; just go with it! Now, tell me the first name that comes to your mind," I told her as I handed her an earring to hold.

"Umm, I don't know. Carol?" she replied.

"Okay, and what else do you get? What do you see?"

"I don't know. An antique office set? Like a desk and some kind of sideboard. And a child's swing set? I don't know. None of this makes any sense," Vicky continued.

"Just keep going."

"All right. I'm also getting the name Judy. I have no idea what any of this means!" She seemed a bit confused and panicked, so I decided to share what she'd just done.

"Okay. You are so much more gifted than you know. I just saw a client named Carol in my office earlier today. I had told her that I saw she'd moved. My furniture in my office is antique, exactly as you described. And her mother's name was Judy. I'm also pretty sure she said she was getting rid of a swing set that was on her property when she bought the new house. You were amazing!"

Vicky couldn't believe what I'd just told her, but I knew to expect that. Clairtangency is an amazing psychic ability and can help open up the rest of your gifts through this form of psychic touch. It was also a great way for her to connect to her clairvoyance.

Try It Now!

Psychometry

Grab a couple of friends and have them bring a few objects. The items can be pictures, or jewelry, or just about anything else that is special either to them or one of their loved ones, alive or dead. As metal tends to hold energy well, this may be a good place to start. Do not share the objects with your friends.

Next, get a hat, or a bag, or something you can drop an object into without anyone looking at it. Also, have plenty of paper and pens handy. Take turns, without anyone seeing, placing the items into the bag. Then, one by one, pick an item out of the bag, trying not to pick your own. Do not look at it, but hold it in your hand. Grab paper and get ready to write down everything you psychically get off of the object.

The point to this exercise, and psychometry in general, is not necessarily to try to guess what the object is that you are holding. Rather, you are just trying to read the energy off of the item. This means you will tune in and let your mind go blank, allowing for a flow of information to begin. To get you started, ask the following questions about how the object makes you feel:

+ Warm or cold?
+ Happy, sad, depressed, excited?
+ Any colors?
+ Sounds?
+ Geographical area or location?
+ Belongs to your friend or someone else?

- Who owns it?
- How was it acquired?
- Special meaning?
- Is the owner or the focus of the object or picture alive or dead?
- Are you picking up any medical or physical ailments or issues?
- Do you get any initials or names?
- Occupations?
- Old, young?
- Married, divorced, single, widowed?
- Any foods they are allergic to?
- Any foods they should stay away from?
- Favorite foods?
- Food that will help them feel good?
- Any flowers that are special to them?
- Anything they are known for?
- Anyone from the other side wishing to say hello?
- If deceased, how did they die?
- If it's a picture, are there people in the picture?
- If so, how many?
- Animal connection?
- Car?
- House, apartment, condo, dorm?

When you are done answering all of these questions about the object you are holding, ask yourself any other questions you may have. Then just sit for at least two minutes, waiting for anything else that needs to be told regarding the item or anyone connected to it. Then draw any pictures, figures, shapes, or even doodles that you feel while holding onto it.

Once you've totally exhausted everything you can think of, have everyone take turns sharing what they've written. Don't let anyone respond until after you are all done sharing. After you have all shared, one at a time, claim the object and have the reader repeat what they wrote, line by line. You can then respond as to whether what they're saying makes sense for your object. Be sure to keep an open mind, however. For example, if someone says they felt a Chinese connection, don't discount it immediately just because you have never been to China. It may just be that you had Chinese food for dinner last night!

After the first person is done validating whatever information they can, it's time to move on to the next person. Then continue with the rest of the objects in the same fashion. You can also mix up the objects and see what other people get for the same item. The objective is to gain as much information as you can, but to just let it come in naturally through your clairtangent senses.

When you are all done, evaluate how you think you did. Were you able to pick up any relevant information? How about any irrelevant but accurate data? Did you receive any pertinent information? Did it feel comfortable? Uncomfortable? Did you feel like you were in the flow of psychic communication? Or did it feel awkward?

If you were way off, don't worry. It may just indicate you need a lot of practice. It also may suggest you might have other, more prevalent, psychic senses and that clairtangence is not necessarily your primary gift. Either way, allow it to be a fun, bonding exercise with your family and friends. Enjoy it!

Now I See Clearly—Combined Gifts

Using all of your clairs will help you tune in better than utilizing only your clairvoyance. It also gives you a fuller picture of whatever it is you are trying to hone in on. Having a broader perspective allows for a clearer interpretation and an increased understanding of exactly what messages you are getting. You may find that using your clairvoyance is the natural way to increase your own psychic abilities, which in turn will create the desire to open up to the other senses more. Having psychic abilities in any combination is what it's all about. Appreciate them and validate them, but above all, celebrate them!

"The language of the brain is symbols..."
—Kevin Todeschi

Chapter Four

Symbols, Signs, and Synchronicities

Being open to messages is only part of the visionary process. Whether using clairvoyant methods or Coordinate Remote Viewing, it's important to acknowledge the impressions we receive symbolically, as these are often the most common way the other side will communicate their messages to us. Recognizing signs as well as symbols creates a clearer understanding of what the universe is trying to tell us. Imagine having a filing cabinet full of symbolic information you can reference instantly, no matter when or why. Learning how to interpret signs and symbols is like having your own personal filing cabinet filled with relevant data for every psychic flash you receive. Receiving symbols is kind of like receiving a shorthand version of a full-on description using a paragraph of information.

Making Symbols Work for You

In my earlier work, *The Book of Psychic Symbols*, I include a general glossary of over five hundred symbols to help the reader interpret psychic messages, dreams, images, and signs. But one of the most important aspects of symbolic interpretation is recognizing that each of us may also have a personal connection to the psychic symbols we receive. "Because there are so many types of symbols, and because a specific symbol can have so many different interpretations, each individual will be the best interpreter of their own images" (Todeschi, 1995). As author Kevin Todeschi explains, we can reference a book about symbols for a general interpretation, but we also need to explore our own memories to see what each one means to us specifically.

Our loved ones and guides from the other side want to communicate with us. They want us to be able to see what they are sharing with us. They need a language we can all speak in order to accomplish this huge task. They need to send their messages as clearly and simply as possibly.

Imagine trying to watch a television show without cable. It's very difficult to tune in to a station well enough to be able to have a clear picture. It's the same with our messengers from the other side. Receiving the message is hard enough, but if you can't interpret it, it's pretty useless. So rather than trying to send us thirty minutes of TV, our etheric helpers may instead send us one image or symbol. Just think about it. How frustrating is it to have your television show interrupted? Now imagine having your psychic messages constantly clouded.

They want us to get it; they are trying to help us. This form of communication is simple, really. By sending us symbolic messages instead of trying to explain things fully, they not only show us something we can relate to but also allow us to apply our own interpretations as well.

When Jane came in a few years ago for a reading, she was looking for answers to some pretty specific questions. "I really just want to know about my house. Is it going to sell? I just can't afford to keep carrying it. I'm upside down on my mortgage, and at this point I can get more for my money if I just rent for a bit. The problem is I don't know where to rent and I don't know if my house will sell," she told me.

Up to this point we had been talking about many different areas of her life and I was able to communicate with her grandfather for her. Through her grandfather I tuned in to a lot, though she wasn't able to validate a few of the things I'd said. I told her I was getting oranges. She said she ate oranges, but they were nothing special. Usually that's a symbol for me of Florida or California. She had no connection to either of these states. I'd also seen images of both a dog and a fish. Again, she had no idea what I was talking about, so we let it go. I just told her to hold onto it and that it may mean something to her later.

"Let's see if I can tune in to your house situation. I'm seeing the oranges, and the dog, and the fish again! I know you didn't understand this before, but does it make any sense now?" I laughed. "Maybe these images are just stuck in my mind!"

"No, I don't get it. They mean absolutely nothing," she replied.

She didn't have quite as much enthusiasm in her response as I'd had in my delivery, so I dug in, trying to give her something she could grasp to help her.

"Well, I can tell you I see your house selling around Thanksgiving, because I'm seeing a turkey," I told her.

"Wow, that's not for like four months. Are you sure it's not going to happen sooner?"

"No, I see like an assembly-line-type machine. That's telling me everything has to line up in order for things to shift. I feel like you're at the beginning stages and the place you'll move to isn't ready for you yet."

"Okay, but I don't know how I'm going to be able to swing this until then."

"Don't worry. It will all work out. I just saw a rainbow. There's a pot of gold on the end. That's a great thing. It means you will do well; there's just a bit of waiting to be done first."

I understood Jane's angst. She was a widow, alone, and on a fixed income that was mostly being taken up by her mortgage and her exorbitant prescription costs. She needed to make changes and was hoping to do it as quickly as possible. She wanted concrete answers and I was only able to provide her with information she wasn't able to easily verify. That is, until later.

It turns out her medicine became more of an ancillary drug, and the cost not only went down, but it was covered in its entirety by her insurance, thus saving her a couple hundred dollars a month. This helped greatly until her home sold in, yes, November, for full price. The next part was very interesting.

"Do you remember what you told me during my reading?" said Jane in a phone message to me.

Now, I honestly rarely remember my readings, regardless of whom they are for and where I've done them. So I called her back and explained. To be frank, I didn't even remember her! I told her as much, not that she wasn't memorable. I believe it's because I see so many people I think my brain would explode if I remembered everything. She giggled and went on to remind me.

"You kept talking about oranges, and a dog, and a fish. I had absolutely no idea what you were talking about. You also said you saw an assembly line and that everything had to be ready and line up in order for things to work."

"Okay..." I encouraged, waiting for more.

"As it turns out, my friend Lorna decided to move to Florida. She'd been thinking about it for quite some time. So she invited me to come and visit her to check out her new condominium. I found out some interesting things when I was there," Jane told me.

"I feel like a little kid waiting to open a present!" I told her, on the edge of my seat.

"I just put a deposit on a brand-new condo in the same complex. It wasn't ready yet! It was still being built. It's very affordable and the timing couldn't be better. And you'll never guess the name of the road."

"I don't know. Orange Lane?"

"No. Dogfish Court! You kept seeing oranges for Florida, a dog, and a fish! Now it makes perfect sense!"

It did make sense. I had seen symbols to indicate exactly when she'd sell her house and where she'd be moving. At the time we just didn't know it yet. Due to my experiences, I knew chances were that the symbols I'd received would mean something to her later on, hence the directive to hold onto them. But most of us don't normally save those images as meaningful if we don't learn to recognize them. This is your chance to start.

Try It Now!

Symbols Journal

Creating a symbols journal helps you to categorize and assimilate symbols into your psychic repertoire and gives you a reference point. It offers you a wealth of information to use for any psychic exercises or any other type of psychic occurrences. It also aids you in interpreting your dreams.

Get a pad, or a journal, or some looseleaf paper you can put into a notebook; first, you are going to create a journal using your conscious mind. You will later add to your journal as you receive symbolic information that you are hoping to interpret or can readily translate.

Start off simply by assigning a symbol to the following objects or words:

- A break-up
- Being sick or ill
- Career
- Driving
- Emailing
- Europe
- Excited
- Family
- Feeling happy
- Losing money or being broke
- Making a lot of money
- Music
- Phone call
- United States
- Vacation

+ Wedding

+ Your friends

+ Your town

When you are all done look back over your symbols. Do they make sense? Were some easier to come up with than others? Was it a tough exercise? Did you enjoy it? Did they come to you right away? Or did you need think about them?

Practice this again using other situations or objects. Do the ones you come up with have more meaning or did they come more easily?

Interpreting Symbols—A Gardening Angel?

When I do readings, I regularly receive symbols as a main form of communication. In the beginning of most of my sessions I explain to my client that I will tell them if I get a symbol, and if necessary, I will tell them what it may mean to them based on my psychic interpretation. I never discount the original symbol, however. Often the symbol holds the message or can even *be* the message.

Heather was not a big believer in psychic ability. She was not expecting to hear anything psychically, nor had she been prepared for the message she received through me. But sometimes the messages just come without asking for them. That's what happens when you are a professional psychic. Usually I can turn it off, but if someone asks me something, it's hard to separate my intuition from my opinion. We were discussing practicalities of work. Heather was talking about wanting to do something different and said she wondered if anything was coming up for her or not.

She had already started her own handygirl business. She was doing all sorts of odd jobs for a variety of customers. This is always tricky because you don't have a set salary or set hours, and it's a constant word-of-mouth-type business.

"I do see you getting offered some business. I'm seeing a wheelbarrow and flowers. To me that has something to do with landscaping or gardening," I told her.

"Hmmm. That would be great. You know I love to work outside and get my hands dirty in the soil," Heather replied.

The images I was seeing were symbolic as well as literal. The wheelbarrow and the flowers represented a particular type of job and I was able to share that with her. I then saw something else.

"Okay, so either you have an angel watching over you or there's something else. I don't know what this means, but I'm seeing, like, a tall angel. Like a statue or something. It's pretty large. And there's also water around it. Maybe it's your guardian angel? Or your gardening angel!"

"Yeah, right. Okay. Guardian angel is pushing it a bit," she laughed.

"Well, like I said, I get the landscaping or gardening thing and I see an angel statue. You can believe it or not—it's totally up to you!" I told her.

"All right. I will let you know when my angel gets me a job!"

I knew there had to be something to what I had seen, though I wasn't quite sure just what it would amount to. After all, Heather was a friend, not a client. We weren't having a full-on hour-long reading. It was just an off-the-cuff thing. I didn't know how accurate it would be, or just what any of it meant, so I let it go and didn't think of it until I talked to her again and she brought it up.

"I don't know how to tell you this. I don't even know if I want to tell you this! I still don't believe. I think it was just coincidence!" Heather said, smiling a strange, somewhat mystified smile.

"Haaa! What? Tell me what? What's going on?" I said.

I'd forgotten all about our previous discussion and what I'd told her. Again, I never seem to remember readings no matter what the forum.

"You told me I would get an offer to do some gardening or landscaping. Well, my mom is a personal assistant. The person she works for had a gardening company do all of her landscaping. She's decided she wants to hire a personal gardener instead. Someone to do all of her work, and she asked if I was interested!"

"Wow," I said.

"Do you remember when you told me about the angel? Do you remember what you said?" she continued.

"No, not really," I answered.

"You told me you saw a tall angel statue or something with water. Do you remember that?"

"Yes, now that you're reminding me," I told her.

"My mom told me that the garden area where she works has a huge angel statue fountain right in the middle of it," she stated.

"Okay…" I said, knowing full well what was going on.

Symbols will show up in many different ways. They come when you need them, to guide you and show you which direction to go. They also come as answers to questions and even answers to prayers. They are shown to you to help explain something in a manner that's easier to understand. Symbols connect you to the other side in such a unique and incredible way that once you begin recognizing them it becomes harder and harder to deny their reality.

Learning what symbols mean is vital to understanding the messages they represent. Some symbols have very common, universal definitions, but others are more personal and carry a more significant meaning. Interpreting them for yourself is key to translating this incredible language we share with the other side.

Try It Now!

Personal Symbols

Take out your new symbols journal that you started in the last exercise. Turn to a fresh page. One at a time, for all of the symbols listed below, write down a definition. Describe in full detail everything each symbol brings to mind. Keep writing for as long as your pen keeps moving. Do not discount anything that comes up. Write it down. You may find that for some of the words you seem to be recording volumes of information, yet for others you may only have a sentence or two.

If you find yourself becoming overwhelmed, break it up. You don't have to finish it all in one sitting. You can split it up and go back to it later. You can even finish it the next day. Either way, give yourself time with each symbol to really appreciate and understand it.

+ Ant
+ Backpack
+ Barn
+ Bathtub
+ Bed
+ Bicycle
+ Bird
+ Book
+ Boy
+ Briefcase
+ Butterfly
+ Cabinet
+ Candle
+ Chair
+ Chalkboard
+ Cheerleader
+ Christmas tree
+ Circus
+ Coffee
+ Computer
+ Cup
+ Cupcake
+ Dog

+ Dragonfly
+ Drawer
+ Fast food
+ Feather
+ Football
+ Girl
+ Glass
+ Grass
+ Hat
+ House
+ Key
+ Lamp
+ Leaf
+ Man
+ Piano
+ Picture
+ Playground
+ Pocketbook
+ Pool
+ Pumpkin
+ Radio
+ Road
+ Rock
+ Rug
+ School
+ Shirt
+ Sneakers
+ Spider

+ Stairway
+ Stove
+ Street sign
+ Table
+ Telephone
+ Television
+ Toaster
+ Toilet
+ Tree
+ Umbrella
+ Vase
+ Wheel
+ Woman

When you have finished giving each symbol a really good, descriptive interpretation, read over what you've written. Does each symbol still hold the same meaning? Do they make even more sense to you now? Are your descriptions about each symbol clear?

Remember, this is your journal, no one else's. The symbolic descriptions need to make sense to you. If you want to compare them to some general or universal meanings, you can reference books such as *The Book of Psychic Symbols*. Books like that are a great way to help with your own impressions. After you've reviewed your entries, add any other symbols that jump out to you. You can also continue this journal indefinitely. Any time you discover a new symbol, amend your personal journal to increase your symbolic knowledge.

Always Symbolic?

The symbols you see will not always be symbolic in the way you expect, but they will always be meaningful. Sometimes they also have double meanings. I did a reading for Joann the other day. When she came in I instantly felt her loved one, and I knew throughout the entire reading that her mother was the one sending me symbols. I was talking about her family and then I saw New York City. I told her I saw her heading into the city and she confirmed she was going in the next week. Then I psychically saw the nuts the street vendors sell.

So I asked her, "Why am I seeing nuts? Is this about your family or the street vendor's nuts and pretzels?"

She laughed and responded that it was both! Her family was in a nutty state and she loved the nuts and pretzels of the street vendors.

When symbols show up, they may have more than one meaning. Don't discredit one over the other. Hold onto it, as I say to my clients. If you can't instantly understand what the symbol is showing you, just keep it in your mind and let it work itself out later.

Signs

Signs and synchronicities are all around us every day, everywhere we look. Once you learn how to recognize them, you'll find they pop up in places where, and at times when, you least expect it. If you are already aware of them, you are probably shaking your head in acknowledgment as you read this!

We all want guidance. We want to be shown, preferably step-by-step, what to do or what will bring us to our greater good. We want to get the most out of life, and if we don't want that, then we *want* to want that. We want it to be relatively easy and have it come to us through more trial than error. We want to succeed and want to know how to succeed. We want the secret.

Guess what? We have the secret! Signs. They tell us what direction to head in and if we are doing the right thing. They help us by confirming or denying that we are moving on the right path or making the right choices.

They are the little coincidences, and the big ones that bring us to where we need to be or admonish us for not paying attention. They are the synchronicities we look to for approval and assurance.

Signs are gifts from our helpers. And they are everywhere. We can actively look for them or they can pop up seemingly out of nowhere. One of my favorite examples is a billboard that simply states, "If you are looking for a sign, this is it." Many of us will ask the universe, "If this is supposed to happen, please give me a sign!" The first time I ever saw that billboard was after I had posed one of these questions.

Signs can be thought of as external symbolic messages. In other words, they are tangible answers to questions or they can be literal images or objects. Recently we were debating whether to get a new car. I'd been enjoying my car without payments and going back and forth about whether it was worth trading it in or keeping it. We'd had some mechanical issues (and still do!), but I still didn't know whether to move forward and get rid of it or not.

You'd think this would have been an easy question, but it really wasn't. For the value, I didn't think I'd get anything as good. I had less than 100,000 miles on it and it was a very safe car for my daughters to not only be in but to also drive. And above all of that, I didn't know whether I wanted to lay out the cash for the deposit and have payments every month. Plus, I actually like my car, when it's running properly.

So, like with everything else in my life, I wanted guidance. I asked for an answer, as I couldn't seem to stop the pendulum feeling of swinging from one extreme to the next. It didn't come for a while. We continued to go back and forth, even driving by dealerships to look at possibilities. Then, when we decided we had to make the call, I asked again:

"Please. If I'm supposed to be rid of this car now, give me a sign to move forward. If I'm supposed to stop looking, I need to know!"

Then I got my answer. Immediately after I'd asked for a sign, I was driving through back roads that I didn't usually travel on. On the right, on the side of the street, I saw a sign almost instantly. It was a large handmade sign that said "SLOW DOWN!" So, being the skeptic I am, I judged it. That couldn't have been my answer, so I asked again.

"If I'm supposed to stop looking, can you please send me another sign?"

Coming around the next bend there was another homemade sign, obviously made by the same people. "YOU ARE GOING TOO FAST!"

Really? Is that the best you've got? "If I'm supposed to cease looking for another car, tell me in plain English!"

Around the corner, there was a narrow overhead bridge. Just before I got to it there was another homemade sign: "STOP!"

Okay, now I got it. There was no denying it. There was no way to avoid the message. Getting a new car was not in the plan for now. I needed to just stop looking. Sometimes when we are not sure of something, we need extreme clarity. That's exactly what happened with me. And luckily, the universe provided it. It was not the right time to get a new car. It would not serve me. I still have my Volvo and it still has some issues, but I do love it.

Try It Now!

Give Me a Sign

There is no prerequisite to asking for signs. All that is required is you ask for one and be ready to receive the answer in whatever form it comes. Think of a question you'd really like an answer to, such as:

+ Will my house sell?
+ Should I stay with my partner?
+ Will I get the job?
+ Should I look for a new job?
+ Is there an end in sight?
+ Will my finances improve?
+ Should I make the move?
+ Is my child picking the right college?
+ Am I picking the right career?

+ Which school should we look at?
+ Should I buy a new car?

Use any of the above or come up with your own question. Be sure to allow plenty of time to receive your answer. Obviously, if you are home with the television and radio off, there will be less of chance to get your sign than if you are out and about. But that doesn't mean it won't happen.

Look for your answer, and if you're not sure you've received it, ask again for more detail. Your sign may come in the form of a song, a street sign, or a message from a friend. It might show up when you're walking your dog or commuting to work. Be open to receiving it, and above all, be ready to acknowledge it! One of the most common ways to miss a sign is to not recognize it when it shows up!

After you've asked for and received a sign for one of your questions, review it. Does it make sense? Is it the answer you expected? Was it shown to you in a way you had anticipated or were you surprised when it showed up? How long did it take to get your sign? Did you need clarification? Did you ask for additional direction?

When you've analyzed the first situation, go for another one! The more you recognize and validate the information the universe sends you, the more apt you are to receive more. Was it easier to recognize the second time around? Did it feel more natural? Or was there still the "aha!" moment when it came? You can ask for signs all the time, but don't depend only on these messages. Apply your own intellect as well—after all, we were provided with a brain for a reason!

Not Always a Sign

Be open to signs. They can show up when you least expect them or when you're looking for them. They can answer questions and give you guidance. They are like getting a gift from the heavens, especially when you need direction. But, remember, not everything is a sign. Assuming everything is a sign will usually leave you feeling disappointed. Rather, expect to see signs, but trust your intuition to know when it really is.

I often get asked, "How do I know it's really a sign?" The answer itself is simple—you will eventually come to distinguish when it is versus when it isn't. Like most things in life, the knowledge doesn't just occur with one hundred percent clarity. Instead, it comes more with familiarity. It is something that you essentially learn to recognize through doing or through experiencing. It is a hands-on type of approach. The more open you are, the more often you recognize signs, and the more natural it will feel. And you will just know in your gut that it has been placed in your path for a reason.

Synchronicities

Signs are the synchronistic events that pop up, and when we recognize them for the guidance they provide, we are all the better for it. *Synchronicities* are what we often call coincidence. Carl Jung coined the term to describe a seemingly random yet related set of occurrences. "Coincidence" is an accidental occurrence, or simultaneous occurrences that randomly happen without forethought or planning. I believe these coincidences are fodder for synchronicity. In other words, these coincidences happen to be recognized as synchronistic events. The saying "there is no such thing as coincidence" is kind of a play on words. Coincidence is synchronistic, and around and around. Coincidence is, therefore, not accidental in the grand scheme of things, making it a synchronistic event.

Right now, as I'm writing, I have my regular radio playing in the background. A song by the band Coldplay is on. I just got a notification from iHeartRadio on my computer that Chris Martin, the lead singer of Coldplay, is about to cover the live show for Ryan Seacrest. The two things, my radio and iHeartRadio, have no connection whatsoever. My radio is tuned to a local station whereas iHeartRadio is an Internet music server. Now, I realize this is not a reason to jump up and down, but this synchronistic event didn't have to happen. Out of the billions of songs and bands, why did it happen to line up this way, with me recognizing it? Synchronicities just happen because they are supposed to; we only need to acknowledge and validate them.

There doesn't always have to be a huge reason for these synchronistic events. Sometimes they are just little nudges to let us know our helpers are around. Other times these synchronicities occur just to make us say "wow." Every now and then, these are the best ones.

We were driving to my daughter Samantha's game last weekend. The game was about an hour away and we were driving down a busy state road, loaded with stores and restaurants as far as the eye could see.

"Oh, I think I went there during one of Molly's dances," I said and pointed to a coffee shop.

We were all surprised by the fact that I not only recognized where we were, but I was pretty sure I'd been there before. We continued down the road, again passing literally over a hundred different stores and restaurants.

"Hmmm. I may have gone there, too. I don't know why that place just popped out at me," I told my family after we'd gone about a mile and a half farther.

There was a restaurant called Moe's. It was one of about five different Mexican restaurants we had passed so far. For some reason it stood out among all the rest, though my memory of actually having ever gone there was totally blank. I decided I must have been there at some point because I couldn't figure out why else it would have been significant enough for me to mention it.

We got to the game. It was at a huge park with picnickers and sports all around. After greeting many of our teammates' families we set up our chairs and sat down. One of our good friends sat with us. We talked about everything and nothing all at once. We were used to having that comfortable banter with Holly. What she said next surprised all of us, but especially me.

"Mandy and I are going to go to lunch after this. We passed a restaurant on the way here and we really want to go. Do you want to come?" she asked.

"Well," I answered, "we were talking about possibly going out to lunch after the game, too, because it's our anniversary!"

I looked to Tom and Molly for their approval. "Do you want to go?" They both said, "Depends on where," at the same time.

That was cute, but it wasn't the funny part. What Mandy said next was.

"Moe's. It's a Mexican restaurant that looked yummy! We passed it on the way here," she replied.

This was not a huge life-altering event, and to be honest, we discovered the food wasn't even all that great. But it was absolutely, most definitely, a synchronistic event. I'd noticed the restaurant for no apparent reason; turns out I had never been there before, but it was significant. It stood out because we were going to go there later. What is interesting is Holly and her daughter pulled into the parking lot for the game behind us, but from a different direction. So, the question is, what came first—the chicken or the egg? Did we put the energy out there for her to notice the restaurant? Or did she pass it first? You may notice this happens often, and trying to figure it out can make you nuts, as it does me.

My husband and I are always doing this. He will randomly say, "Did you hear from Molly?" and I will respond that I just texted with her. Or he'll ask, "Is Samantha coming home for dinner?" and I'll tell him she just asked if she could eat at her friend's house. So, which happened first? Did my communicating with the kids trigger his question? Or did his thinking about the question trigger my communicating? These are the random synchronistic episodes that, although not huge, are wondrous. They always, every time, make us ponder who thought of it first. In other words, was one of us the sender and the other the receiver? Or did it occur at the same time? And more importantly, does it matter? The universe made it happen. It was supposed to happen. Maybe just so we are able to acknowledge it.

Incredibly, again, I just got a notification on my phone that I had a message. When I picked it up I accidentally pressed the button to go into my Twitter account. The first entry on my Twitter feed read, "Coincidence???" Now why on earth would that have happened?

Try It Now!

Synchronized

When was the last time you had a synchronistic experience? Have you ever recognized having one? Get out your symbols journal and move about halfway into the middle, leaving plenty of room for your personal symbols, but giving yourself enough room to create a synchronicities journal as well. It's time to acknowledge your synchronicities by recording them.

The first thing you need to do is determine what type of situations or events may produce synchronicities. Write these down. You may find that you have listed multiple different situations or you may only have a couple. Before you move on, be sure you've written down anything you can regarding when or where a synchronistic event can happen. Only when you are all done writing should you move on and read what comes next.

Guess what? The opportunities for synchronistic events to occur are infinite! There is no limit to how, when, or even why these incredible coincidences happen. If you wrote that down, you are right on track. If not, no worries! You are still on your way to understanding them.

Now, take your journal and list any synchronicities you've experienced that you can remember. Write down what they were. Also write who you were with, where you were, how soon after it the realization hit you that it was a synchronicity, and how you felt when you acknowledged it for what it was. Then search your memory for any additional events.

After you've completed that, write down any beginnings of synchronicities that you've wondered about or noticed. For example, I noticed Moe's Restaurant for some reason but didn't know why it was significant. But the important thing was that I wondered why it stood out. That would be the beginning of a synchronicity. You may experience times like this that have no real basis to be anything more than a passing notice, but they may prove to be more. Write those down. By recording them you are allowing the synchronicity to have the space to occur. You are ready to acknowledge it to the universe. Just write it down, leaving plenty of room, and let it go.

Then be open to having the other half play out. When it does, be sure to enter it into your journal. You may begin to notice more and more synchronistic events happening. They may become bigger and more important, or even crucial to whatever experiences you are having. They might just be an answer to your particular situation. Remember, there is no wrong way to do this. Just record what feels right; don't worry if it doesn't come to fruition.

Common Sense and Synchronicity

As with everything psychic, a bit of common sense must be applied. This basically means that cultivating your relationship with your gifts has to be done with thought and inquisitiveness. In other words, don't assume every single thing is a synchronistic or extrasensory event. But at the same time, don't ignore your intuition. Instead, know that you are here to live a life filled with a variety of surprises; some of them will be ordinary, but hold onto your hat, because some will indeed be extraordinary!

"Sometimes seeing is believing."
—Unknown

Chapter Five
Now Do You See?

Learning to see with your third eye is as easy or as difficult as you want to make it. There really aren't many rules; there is only guidance. The only real rule is that you allow it to happen. Seeing is believing, but that doesn't always mean you need to see externally. With psychic ability comes faith that what's happening is real or that what you're seeing is at least a possibility.

With psychic gifts becoming increasingly prevalent in today's society, there is more of a reason to expand your own awareness. Not because you need to stay ahead of the game or even because you need to keep up with Joneses. Rather, you deserve to understand and partake in this amazing gift of conscious knowing; it is a natural part of each and every one of us. World-renowned medium and author James Van Praagh believes this too. As he states in his book, *Heaven and Earth: Making the Psychic Connection,* "We are all spiritual beings on a journey to enlightenment" (Van Praagh, 2001).

Multitudes of people are opening up to the idea that there is more to life than what most of us have previously acknowledged. After all, are we naïve enough to think life began and will end with us? Or that the millions of people who have experienced psychic connections with departed loved ones, angels, or guides are *all* making it up? We know this is not the case. We are an informed population and we are knowledge seekers. We gather information to gain wisdom, and even to use as ammunition when necessary, when defending our beliefs becomes more important than simply believing in them.

Try It Now!

I Believe

For this exercise you are simply going to affirm what you are learning to believe in. You've done so much work already and performed so many exercises that, along the way, you've undoubtedly decided to believe, at least, in the possibility that you have only just begun to tap into your own psychic vision. Throughout this book and the rest of your life you can reiterate these words any time you need to feel capable or empowered. Say the following words aloud, and then repeat them in your mind at least three times:

I believe in multiple possibilities.
I believe there is more to life than what the naked eye can see.
I believe I am able to see things more clearly
by using my clairvoyant abilities.
I believe in psychic vision and all it has to offer.
I am learning to utilize these gifts in a safe
and fun environment and will share them when warranted.
I believe.

How It Feels to Believe

Decoding the language of our intuition is something we've done as long as we've been alive. Living by gut instinct kept the first humans alive; they knew when to move on and when to stay, or who to trust even when there was no written or generally understood vernacular. This has been demonstrated time and time again. Police officers use their gut instinct; mothers do, too. Even financial wizards rely on more than just research and tend to direct their investments to where they feel drawn.

Knowing when to use our intuition is easy. Use it whenever it feels right! My basic rule of thumb is to use your psychic ability when you feel you need to, and use your intellect as well. They are adjunct functions—not opposites. It doesn't have to be *either/or*, it is *and*. Understanding that will get you further than relying solely on one or the other. To ignore one or the other could actually cause you grief, as it would go against your natural inclinations.

I was at a lacrosse tournament the other day and had the opportunity to meet some very interesting people. We talked about the basics: the frigid temperature we would have to endure throughout the day, the different towns we were coming from, how long our kids had been playing lacrosse, and intuition. The concept that we may look into the future and see with some clarity the possible order of events that are coming up in our lives is a thing to celebrate. Being able to see what a person's true intentions are in any type of relationship would be incredible. Being able to tune in to and see your loved ones and receive their messages through psychic sight is an amazing gift that nobody would trade. Knowing how to tap into that psychic sight seems to be the only thing holding most people back. Well, that and the embarrassment of admitting to others that they believe in it.

Many people are afraid to declare what they think to be true. Part of the problem is that they aren't always perfectly clear in their convictions. Not knowing exactly what it is they believe in can hold them back from being assured in their own truths. Discussing psychic vision with the people I met this past weekend created a depth of understanding, which in turn instilled additional confidence that the clairvoyant experiences they've had that they weren't previously able to completely believe in were indeed real. Understanding that this is their personal path to follow has allowed them the luxury to not worry about negative repercussions from anyone who may not yet be at their level of psychic vision. Once they realize that, they feel good about their intuitive abilities.

Out of the blue one day, my husband said to me, "I am very proud of you."

I had absolutely no idea what he was talking about or what he meant by it, so I asked him, "What do you mean? Why?"

"Because you work so hard at what you do. You give clients what they need and you do it with a smile," he answered.

"Awww. That's nice. Thanks!" I replied, thinking it really wasn't a big deal.

But he continued. "I'm proud of you because not only do you help others, but you do it without fear of being touted as foolish. It's hard enough to have your own business, but to put yourself out there as a practicing psychic when so many people don't believe in what you do, and may even go so far as to think you're a bit crazy, is amazing to me."

That melted my heart. For him to not only recognize and acknowledge what I deal with as my reality but also to be so supportive was fantastic. I am lucky. I am able to put aside others' disbelief and even their challenges. I know my path is not the same as everyone else's. However, for others who aren't so clear in their convictions, the fear of looking foolish to their peers can hold them back from truly connecting to their clairvoyance. Unfortunately, this can hinder the psychic process. Again, no other person lives your life and no one can tell you what you see and what you don't. Devaluing your psychic vision doesn't mean it's not real; it just cheats you out of what can be incredible experiences.

The reality is, though you've gone through many of the exercises in this first part of the book, you probably won't be ready or eager to hang your psychic shingle and advertise yourself as the newest clairvoyant. However, you have hopefully become more acquainted with the gifts you may have. Psychic vision, remember, is enhanced by encouraging your other intuitive vibes to kick in and enrich your clairvoyance. Regardless of which clair ability you use to tune in, it's all part and parcel in your journey to see beyond the sights the naked eye can bring you.

Try It Now!

Your Favorite Exercise

You've done numerous exercises throughout part one. You may feel as though you exceeded your expectations with a particular one, or possibly you had a difficult time with one more than the others. In this exercise, you will go back to one of the exercises and do it again. Pick either the exercise you did really well or the exercise you had the hardest time with, and perform it again as though you haven't done it before. If you are so inclined, go ahead and do both!

Did you pick the challenging one? Did you pick the easier one? How did it feel to do it again? Did it come out the same? Did you end up with different results? Did you do better? Did you do worse? If you did both exercises, did they switch places, with the more difficult one becoming the one you excelled at? Was it more comfortable than the first time? Did it feel uncomfortable? If the exercise called for you to record or use your journal, did you find you wrote more details than during the initial attempt? Or less?

When you are all done answering the above questions, write down any of the other exercises you'd like to do again. Did you choose any that you previously felt less confident with? Or did you pick only ones you liked? If you want, go ahead and do all of the exercises again!

Absolutes? Only If You're Present

When I was a child, we had a ghost named Henry who roamed the stairwell in our house in Wilton, Connecticut, and was a convenient scapegoat for everything that went missing or was still messy when Mom got home from working a double shift at the hospital. At the time, I thought Henry was a figment of my imagination. Actually, I believed he was more of a shared, fictional creation that we blamed things on in order to lighten the mood when something was wrong. I didn't realize that he was actually a ghost, someone from the other side who was repeating his walk up and down the stairs on a regular basis.

Sometimes we just can't be sure that we are absolutely experiencing psychic visions. It makes perfect sense; after all, not much in life is guaranteed. If I had been asked way back then, when I was about ten years old, I would have said, "We absolutely do not have any ghosts in our house. I absolutely do not see anything." I never knew that I was psychically seeing someone whom the rest of my family openly acknowledged seeing. Now that I have had more experience and was able to compare notes many years later, I am certain that I absolutely did see Henry, that he was real, and that I used my clairvoyance to see him.

Just because we aren't able to consistently produce indisputable evidence of our psychic visions does not make them any less real. By the same token, those instances don't always need proving. We need to be humble enough that we can allow room in our lives for them to continue to occur. We are not always in charge of what we see psychically, though we can be in control of recognizing the value in our clairvoyant gifts. It can actually be astounding when we realize there are so many practical applications that can prove beyond measure when we use our psychic sight.

Once we've determined there are no absolutes, we can better understand the need to always be present. Being present and in the moment permits us to remain humble and appreciate when we do experience a random psychic vision. Dr. Seuss may have said it best when he said, "Sometimes you will never know the value of a moment until it becomes a memory." Live now, not in the past, and not in the future if you desire psychic guidance. You need to be present or you won't be able to experience it for yourself.

This Vision Is All For You

Your clairvoyance is *your* gift. It's all the proof you need that psychic vision exists and that you can tap into it to help you decipher upcoming events, communications from the other side, and even current situations. These psychic discoveries can be of extreme importance or they can pertain to common, everyday things. There is no limit to what you can use your clairvoyant abilities for as long as you abide by your own code of morals. Ethically you don't want to invade anyone's privacy with your intuitive gifts, just as you wouldn't want them to overstep their boundaries with you. You are well on your way to developing your psychic vision and your own personal transformation.

Still need more proof that we have the ability to gain information from distant locations, times, objects, people, and places? Keep reading! The next section will help you understand these incredible abilities from a more structured and scientific viewpoint. Need more practice? Again, keep going! The two approaches are indeed different, but can yield many of the same results. And always remember—you always have the option to use both! The amazing author C.S. Lewis said, "There are far, far better things ahead, than any we leave behind" (*Collected Letters of C. S. Lewis*, 2006). Tomorrow is the first day of the rest of your amazing psychic life. Enjoy what is to come rather than trying to prove to others what is already here.

Part Two

COORDINATE REMOTE VIEWING

"The secret is out: remote viewing exists, it works, it has been
tested, proven, and used in intelligence for ... decades."
—David Morehouse

Chapter Six

Coordinate Remote Viewing— In the Beginning

Seeing Myself

I didn't like it at all. I was angry. I was sad. I was confused. But more than that, I wanted it to end. I kept feeling like there was someone looking over my shoulder. The entire evening, clear through the morning, I couldn't shake the notion that someone was watching me. I'd also been seeing strange things in my mind's eye. I'd been seeing ladybugs ever since I'd left the classroom. And the food that I usually loved from the dining hall seemed to be overrun by big, fat, juicy, bright-green caterpillars that appeared to be smiling up at me. This was not going well.

And why now was I also seeing in my mind the fencing and the woods that were all around me at Omega, a school and workshop center for holistic studies in Rhinebeck, New York? And my hair, too. Why was it that I felt I knew exactly what my hair looked like in the back? And, even more bizarre, why did it take me so long to process simple things? Okay, so the person in the bathroom stall in my dormitory for the week was standing up, facing the toilet to use the bathroom instead of sitting like I was. Why was that so incredibly strange to me? Maybe because it took me a good five minutes to process that it was, indeed, a coed dorm. And why, oh why, did it feel like there was a shadow following me?

Most importantly, why did I feel helpless to change any of it? How come I was quietly weeping as I made my way back into the classroom that next morning, hoping to put an end to what was obviously the strangest night I'd ever spent at my favorite location? My sleep had been infiltrated by visions, which kept me awake for the better part of the evening. I did note, however, that I liked the image of the curly haired, cherubic head that seemed to float in front of me on occasion, both in my dreams and upon waking, and even though the ladybugs and cater-pillars seemed like an infestation, they made me happy. I knew there was more to this, yet the question remained—was I the target?

Walking into the beautiful, large, open classroom, I could feel the air and the woods making their way inside through the huge windows and doors. It almost felt like we were in a tree house. As everyone else filed in, took off their shoes, and found a place to sit, I noticed they were all, for the most part, cheerful. There seemed to be no evidence of any of the distress I'd been enduring. They displayed no sadness or feelings of vul-nerability or frustration like I'd encountered throughout the overnight. Yet I definitely felt like I'd truly done the exercise and done it well. Of that I had no doubt.

The year was 2006, and I was taking a certification course to become a Certified Coordinate Remote Viewer. I'd been at the center for about a week and had been enjoying myself immensely with about ten other students. We'd been training with an ex-CIA operative and highly deco-rated Army officer who'd been part of the United States government's top-secret Stargate program. I took this class because I wanted to dive deeper into psychic awareness and put some scientific fact behind what I already knew to be true. Little did I know I was in for a life-changing week. I discovered that though I believed in the very precise process of Coordinate Remote Viewing, I also knew without any doubt that it was essentially the same thing as what I did using my psychic vision or clair-voyance. "In classic terminology remote viewers are psychics" (Smith,

2014). But they (my teacher and the government) insisted that Coordinate Remote Viewing was not psychic, nor would it ever be classified as psychic. Because, you see, it was regimented and structured, and surely that was not psychic. Well, that was actually all right with me, because whatever it was, it was captivating.

Throughout the week we'd been exposed and trained in the government's version of psychic espionage. There were strict guidelines to be adhered to in order see targets: to "transcend time and space, to view persons, places, or things remote in time and space … and to gather intelligence information on the same" (Morehouse, 1996). Though the venue and the status were different, we were assured that the methodology and the basic directions were the exact same as what was used by those who were part of the CIA's Stargate program, also known as Sun Streak. And it was fascinating.

The last target, the one I'd been fretting over all night long, was about to be revealed. Our teacher, David Morehouse, told us we had accomplished so much in so little time. We'd been able, for the most part, to tune in to the Coordinate Remote Viewing (CRV) targets, and, using the pre-directed instructions, to bring back information that we were able to qualify and quantify based on the details we saw. He asked us what we thought the target was. Some guessed, albeit incorrectly, but nevertheless they tried.

"Was it the US Open? I saw a lot of people," said one student.

"What about Nigeria? I felt like I was home," someone else answered.

"Was it the inside of my car?" asked another.

To all of these, and more, the answer was no. That's not what the selected target had been; however, they were also correct in a way.

"I believe it was more personal. I kept feeling like someone was with me, directly behind me, looking over my shoulder. It made me very, very uncomfortable. I didn't like the feeling at all and I was very frustrated because I felt like there was no making the target any better or any healthier. It just was. I was even weepy, though I wasn't sure why. Was the target here? At Omega? Was I the target?" I asked him as everyone looked at me strangely.

He then went on to let us know that we, indeed, *were* the targets. Each one of us. He had given us the coordinates and the assignment was ourselves.

Well, that explained it all right. Throughout the entire evening I had been following myself. That clarified the sensation of someone looking over my shoulder and of feeling like it took me twice as long to figure things out. I realized then that the ladybug represented my daughter, Molly, as we always called her "Our Molly Bug" and attached that to images and thoughts of ladybugs. The green juicy caterpillar represented my younger daughter, Samantha, because she was bursting at the seams with energy and filled with vibrancy and healing. I also came to discover that the cherubic, grandmotherly image I'd been seeing is one of my guides, who I can now call on to help me see things psychically. At the time of the workshop I'd been going through some medical issues, which also explained why I felt unable to fix myself. It all made perfect sense now.

This assigned target was one of many we had the chance to work on during my certification course. All of the targets were designated by our instructor and were not pre-disclosed to any of us. We learned how to tune in to these targets using a very clear-cut, precise method designed to expose elements of the target without having to jump immediately to knowing what the target actually was.

Try It Now!

Who Are You?

Imagine you are remote viewing yourself. Look around you and pay attention to where you are.

+ What do you see?
+ What details are there?
+ How would you describe any objects around you?
+ Who else is there?

- What stands out to you?
- Do you see yourself?

    If so, what do you notice?

    Hair?

    Clothing?

    Shoes?

    Skin color?

- Do you feel any emotion?

How It All Started

Coordinate Remote Viewing works differently than clairvoyance because there is a very specific protocol that has been created to perform it, based on scientific research done by physicists as well as mentalists and psychics. Aristotle said, "Intuition is the source of scientific knowledge." The methods used to tune in to the targets are the same across the board, no matter whether or not the sitter (the practitioner of the Coordinate Remote Viewing) has any previous experience or any psychic ability. The United States government set about developing this program in response to discovering another country's *psychotronic* research.

Though my experiences during my remote viewing training were amazing and personal to me as an individual and as part of a group, the initial intent of the remote viewing program was not to be used for fun, or as a sideshow act, or strictly for amusement. Rather, the program was created to combat the discovery of the Soviet Union's own mind-energy applications and to determine whether it was merely psychic nonsense or a true threat to America's national security.

Upon finding out the Soviet Union was developing their own version of psychic espionage during the years 1969–1971, the Central Intelligence Agency (CIA) funded a program to determine the validity of remote viewing and research and evaluate its use as an intelligence tool. Physicists Harold Puthoff and Russell Targ were contracted to conduct and carry out research at the Stanford Research Institute (SRI) in 1972. They utilized such gifted and talented psychics as Uri Geller and the co-creator of remote viewing, Ingo Swann. It was through these innovators, and more, that the Stargate program was developed.

Originally known as SCANATE, the remote viewing program was directed at times by, and part of, the Army, the CIA, the Defense Intelligence Agency (DIA), and the private sector where the technology was developed further through Psi Tech and SRI. It naturally progressed and grew into future endeavors known as Gondola Wish, Grill Flame, Center Lane, Sun Streak, and eventually Stargate. During the various stages of research, discovery, and applied targeting, remote viewing produced erratic results when looked at from a purely skeptical viewpoint. But, when analyzing where the $20 million–plus was spent, the results are much more promising, if not conclusive. The psychic warfare we engaged in was well worth the money in part because it helped locate various kidnapped military and state department personnel, as well as discovering at least one specific KGB spy. (The KGB was the highly secretive, secluded security agency for the Soviet Union from 1954 until its collapse in 1991.) Remote viewing has also been successfully employed to uncover and expose threats to our country, including missile-grade submarines, SCUD missiles, various underground military facilities, and chemical and biological weapons.

Ingo Swann released a statement on December 1, 1995, addressing the basis of remote viewing. After being inundated by reporters and others asking for explanations, he decided to address the fundamentals of military involvement and the efficiency of remote viewing. Previously to (and causing him to offer) his account, the CIA made an official statement regarding remote viewing; in September 1995, the CIA briefly admitted to the media and general public that the government did, indeed, invest in this controversial and speculative research.

In November 1995, ABC's television show *Nightline* ran a story with anchor Ted Koppel that he announced as "Psychic Spies: Cold War Whimsy or Secret Weapon?" He opened up by stating, "We live in an age of once unimaginable miracles, so it would take equal measures of courage and hubris to dismiss as impossible the notion that some people may have certain psychic powers. This may reassure you, it may alarm you, but in fact for some years now the US intelligence community has wagered a modest amount of money on the possibility that such powers do exist."

Ted Koppel's *Nightline* exposé revealed the existence of the government's remote viewing effort. The show included interviews with former CIA directors Robert Gates, Dale Graff, Edwin May, and Joe McMoneagle. Also interviewed was a man who was heavily involved in the remote viewing program, and who was simply called Norm. The gist of the *Nightline* show ran the gamut from "remote viewing doesn't work" to "remote viewing produces incredible results." When asked about their findings, each interviewee had a slightly different answer. Norm, however, talked about the eight-martini sessions. Ingo Swann cleared up what this meant in his own statement: "What, then, is an 'eight-martini' result? Well, this is an intelligence community in-house term for remote viewing data so good that it cracks everyone's realities. So they have to go out and drink eight martinis to recover."

Soon after, in December 1995, the CIA canceled the Stargate program, essentially ceasing all government involvement and spending in this arena. This left it wide open for the private or public sector to dive in and discover all of the benefits and uses for remote viewing. This is when I learned about remote viewing as it was originally taught.

Now What?

Everyone can learn to remote view, even if you've never had any inclination toward psychic abilities. Will everyone be great, or even good, at it? No. Just like how not everyone who plays football will play in the Super Bowl and not every actor will be a movie star, not everyone who trains in remote viewing will be accurate. But everyone can be trained in the process. So what makes a good viewer? As Joseph McMoneagle, the original Remote Viewer 001, said in his book *Remote Viewing Secrets*, "Experience dictates that it's probably a mixture of desire and focus (33 percent), quality and intensity of training (33 percent), and the natural talent you walk in the door with (33 percent)" (McMoneagle, 2000).

I want to be clear—I was never part of the original Stargate program or any part of the original CRV research. I've never served in the military or any branch of government. I've never trained directly with or been studied by SRI. I was lucky enough, however, to have been educated and trained in the classic Coordinate Remote Viewing protocol by a retired Army Major who was.

I am a Certified Coordinate Remote Viewer. Does being certified in remote viewing mean I'm psychic? No, not according to the program the United States government created. The DIA has been using psychic espionage for over forty years, though most people are not aware of this. They have developed a scientific—yes, scientific—way to access information distant in time and space. And it works. Now we are lucky enough to be introduced to this very distinct system.

Since its inception, remote viewing has morphed from focusing mainly on military targets and explorations to more personal endeavors, such as possible financial futures, job possibilities, missing people, and even assisting the police in finding murderers and criminals. The protocol, originally developed by SRI, really cannot be fully taught simply by reading a book. Years of research, thousands of training hours, and multiple practice targets were accumulated by the original government and SRI viewers. The methods in this book are only a representation of the once+classified protocols. As Joseph McMoneagle says in another of his books, *Memoirs of a Psychic Spy*, "Regardless of the method used, a method is never considered an acceptable substitute for the protocol" (McMoneagle, 2006). Yet we, the general public, will not work in the now-disbanded Stargate program, so we will utilize the procedures passed down from those who have. From these methods you will in essence learn how to remote view as I, and thousands before you, have.

Where Does the Information Come From?

With psychic sight or clairvoyance, we receive our information from the other side. For example, it's common to get messages from the universe, God, angels, our deceased loved ones, spirit guides, etc. All events in all of time are out there to be discovered by tuning in to the energy of the universe. The scientific background of CRV is very similar to this, but with a twist.

Imagine our existence along a timeline. Start with what we believe as the beginning of time and go all the way to this moment, right now. Then, imagine folding that timeline over itself and backward; this is known as a signal line. Essentially, time is insignificant; there is no time that cannot be revisited. The concept of time is irrelevant, as every moment in time can be tuned in to along the signal line, as it is all part of the matrix. The matrix, essentially, is what we know as the universe. It is tiny, little particles all allied and interspersed throughout what we know as reality and what we only dream about. It is the point of origin from which everything develops or takes form, and is therefore connected to everything, everyone, and every moment in time. The matrix is a framework of information that is accessible to everyone; what I refer to as the universal energy, and what Carl Jung called the collective unconscious, in remote viewing is called the matrix. The signal line emerges from the matrix to bring forth information during the CRV session. It is this signal line we are able to tap into to perform the procedures to come, to be Coordinate Remote Viewers.

"Content be damned...
Structure is everything."

—from the walls of the Remote Viewing Unit
in Fort Meade, Maryland

Chapter Seven
Coordinate Remote Viewing — Stage I

The Structure

Protocols are put in place for a reason. They are there to keep order and to keep methodology consistent. Scientists are very precise, and the ones at SRI who originally helped design and create remote viewing were no different. The system they built was continually tested, over decades, with people known to have psychic abilities as well as lay people who never showed a hint of possessing any level of intuition. The testing proved that remote viewing was real and had value. The methods they created are what we use today.

Coordinate Remote Viewing is a very specific method of tuning in to an object, place, or person distant from the psychic or viewer in time and space. It is different than tuning in to your third eye or your clairvoyance. Remote viewing, at its fundamental base, requires the psychic and anyone else in the room to be blind to any of the target data. This typically is different from clairvoyant or psychic readings, because usually the person you are reading for is with you and aware of their own life and those in it. CRV is done in stages. There are six basic stages plus a session summary. Each of the steps is important, none more so than the others, but you can do a shortened version by only doing the first three.

Originally designed with a human monitor present, this scientific form of remote viewing was created to take advantage of having someone there with the viewer to keep track of and observe how the viewer was responding to the data they were receiving. The other person is also there to provide help should the viewer become distressed, or to help the viewer acquire the site. They are there to observe but also guide without using leading terminology. The monitor can also help to recognize any body language, etc., that is present, which may indicate a need to declare and objectify some type of interruption (see chapter eight). This is still the preferred method of performing a CRV session, but is rarely the case when not in a scientific, military, or even a group setting.

You may find that learning this process with a friend will be beneficial. First, you will have fun—imagine being able to share this with someone who is just as invested in the process as you. The experiences you have together will increase your excitement and can even enhance your learning potential. Second, you can work on the same targets by having someone else dictate the coordinates to you both, giving you a fuller, more advanced look at the target data before you receive feedback. Third, you can take turns monitoring one another, gently leading each other through a session and offering positive advice and feedback as to the methodology and structure each person is using.

Now On to the How

The first step in remote viewing is to write your name, the date, and the start time. This seems to be a simple step, but as I've stated, there is very specific protocol that needs to be followed. It looks like this on the top right corner of the paper:

Wanda See
7/12/14
ST: 2:47 pm
ET:*
*this is blank until you are done with the session

So far, so good. This is easy to understand. The next step isn't too difficult either. Preconceptions or advanced visuals (AV) are listed next. These are any images or thoughts that are stuck in your mind or that are there before you begin. They can be what you are thinking the target may be or something as irrelevant as what you had for breakfast. Nothing is insignificant, however, so these need to be recorded. Writing whatever is in your mind helps to dump those thoughts or images so you can move on. You will want to declare "yes," and then describe any AVs, or state "no" and move on.

Directly below that you are going to record any Physical or Personal Inclemencies (PI). These are conditions that may alter or prevent information you receive during your session from the signal line. As described earlier, the signal line is the connection to the matrix, or the universal energy that connects all of us that is used to connect to the target data. List here anything you are experiencing, including but not limited to headaches, feeling grumpy, toothaches, colds, exhaustion, menstrual cycle or cramping, hangovers, stress, etc. Again, as with the AVs, you want to list any of these here to help prevent any distortion of your viewing session or coloring of the information you are receiving.

This section is not designed to be a huge part of the CRV session. Acknowledge your AVs and PIs and move on—don't write a book about them. The structure to record these items is to list them in the center of the page:

Advanced Visuals or Perceptions (AV)
If yes, describe them. Otherwise, write no and move on.

Physical or Personal Inclemency (PI)
If yes, list them. Otherwise, write no and move on.

The example below is what the beginning of a Coordinate Remote Viewing session would look like. Again, the AVs and PIs will vary from person to person, day to day, and even moment to moment.

Wanda See
7/12/14
ST: 2:47 pm
ET:

AV- yes/ popcorn and a beach, water

PI- yes/ tired, right knee hurts, missing my dog

Try It Now!

Getting Started with Coordinate Remote Viewing

Get out a piece of paper and a pen, and relax. You are not going to run through an entire remote viewing session, so you don't really need to do any other preparation. On the top right corner of the paper write down your name, the date, and the current time. Underneath that write "ET," which stands for "end time," leaving space to fill in after the session is completed.

Then go ahead and list your AVs and PIs in the center of the sheet, directly underneath your personal data. When you are all done, go back up and fill in the end time.

What have you recorded? What AVs, if any, did you describe? What PIs, if any, did you list? By putting them down on paper you are acknowledging them, but you are also allowing your mind to be rid of them so you can move on.

Stage I

Let's talk *gestalt*. This means that the sum of the parts does not always equal the whole. This is true when defining the gestalt of the target. The *DIA Remote Viewing Manual* was a cumulative manual produced by the SRI and CIA to describe and teach the CRV methods. This manual states, "The gestalt of a target site is what makes the target uniquely what it is ... The overall impression presented by all elements of the site taken for their composite, interactive meaning" (*Remote Viewing Manual*, 1986). It is the gestalt, or the overall impression of the whole of the site, that is the goal of remote viewing. This holds true if the target is a location, person, place, thing, or event. Stage I, executed properly, provides the foundation with which to achieve this objective.

And the Coordinates Are ...

The initial step in Stage I is writing down coordinates that are assigned to the target. Random coordinates are given to the viewer that are relevant to the target data. The viewer has no previous knowledge of the target data or the coordinates. Originally, when the CRV program was in its infancy stage, the coordinates used were actual map coordinates. The problem, however, was that most of the CRV participants were military personnel with training to recognize the locations specified. So, since realizing the actual coordinates were merely a tool used to designate a target, it was determined that the intention was what was meaningful, and not the actual map coordinates. They then did away with using actual map coordinates.

So they were left with a commonly applied method to assign the numbers. These numbers are generally derived as a series of eight numbers, four over four. Often, the first four are the year and the next four are totally made up, with the idea that they will pinpoint the target within a specific time frame. For example, if your objective was the Statue of Liberty, the coordinate numbers could be 2014 and 9367. Or they could be 2014 and 8015, or they could be 6295 and 7593. It really doesn't matter what the second series, or even the first series, of numbers are—it's about the intent. Whoever is applying the coordinates does so with the intent that they represent the specific target being researched. These coordinates are written down in the left third of the paper under the AVs and PIs.

Try It Now!

Coordinate It

Think of something you'd like to target and get out your journal.

Is it a person? A place? A thing?

What is your target? Are you intending for your target to be viewed in:

Present time? Past time? Future time?

If you know of a specific date or even year, relevant to your target, when is it? Now, what are some possible coordinates? Remember to list them one on top of the other.

Great! You have just assigned your first target area! You don't need to do anything further with it. This was simply an exercise to understand how the coordinates are formulated.

Creating an Ideogram

The *ideogram* is an essential part of the process. It is the first initial connection to the coordinates. After writing down the coordinates, the next step is to allow a reflexive response through the muscles of the arm as you hold your pencil, down through the hand, which creates an ideogram. This is a line drawing that feels like the target, but is drawn strictly as a result of placing the pencil to the paper. It is the first real connection you have to the signal line—where the information comes from out of the matrix or the universe. For beginners it's easiest to produce the ideogram as a single line mark. It is possible to create ideograms with double lines, multiple lines, or a composite made up of many lines connected by breaks. We will be focusing initially on the single line, as that is more than adequate for tuning in to any target data.

The ideogram is sometimes done in the center of the paper, but often it is directly connected to the coordinates, beginning as soon as the last number is completed. Either way, the ideogram is executed without thinking, without a time lapse in between, and strictly as an automatic, spontaneous, reflexive action.

Assuming the coordinates of 2014 and 9367, the following is an example of a spontaneous ideogram. The loop that is part of the ideogram is not necessarily a normal part of all ideograms. Each ideogram is independent and unique.

Ideogram with Coordinates

Try It Now!

Ideograms

Get out a piece of blank paper; make sure it's plain, unlined paper. You don't need any practice for this exercise; you need only start. When you are ready, place your pen on the left third section of the paper. This is the cueing position. Listed below are ten sets of coordinates. One at a time, record the coordinates and immediately let your pen move across the paper, creating an ideogram.

You may find some coordinates flow easier than others, but don't let this bother you. You may also find some will be more horizontal in nature and some may have more of a vertical slant. Again, don't focus on this. It's not important. What is important is that you let the pen run its course without thinking about it. Do not concentrate on what the ideogram does or does not look like. Don't focus on how your hand feels. Just write the coordinates down and immediately, without hesitation, allow the automatic reflex to occur, creating your ideogram. Above all, relax! This is the beginning of a whole new way of viewing for you!

Here we go!

2014
3597

2014
4371

2014
7590

1760
2148

5431
2467

2014
4309

2015
3825

2015
1423

2015
7277

2015
3298

When you are done, look at your ideograms. How do they look? Do they appear similar to each other or different? Are they horizontal, or vertical, or both? Do they contain any loops or swirls? Are there points or are they smooth? Did one flow easier than the others? Was one more difficult?

The ABCs of Ideograms

Stage I is commonly known as the I/A/B/C stage. The "I" is for ideogram, which you've just practiced. After you've allowed your ideogram to flow onto your paper, it's time for the "A," "B," and "C" components. All three of these have something in common—they are based on the feel of the ideogram.

The "A" component is the "motion" of the ideogram. It's about how you felt or the sensation you experienced when producing the ideogram itself. This is where you briefly describe the impression of the ideogram, meaning the shape, the contour, and the motion of the target site, which is translated through the ideogram. Using the same ideogram as before, you might interpret the motion as below:

Ideogram with Coordinates

A. Slow rise up, curving around, straight down, curving under, angle rising, arching over, sloping down, flat, angled down

Remember, the feeling of the target site is what's significant with the "A" component. The point to this phase of Stage I is to describe the motion characteristics of the ideogram. The reflexive action that caused the spontaneous mark to manifest is directly connected to the target data. It is this energy that you are translating through the "A" component.

If you have trouble feeling the motion of the ideogram, you can probe the line. To do this simply put your pen on the beginning of the line and begin tracing the ideogram by placing dots along its path. As you are probing the line, you may find the feeling of the shape or contours of the target site becomes clearer. Write the feelings of the ideogram down as they come.

Try It Now!

Ideogram A: Assessing the Motion

Using the same ideogram from the previous practice, go ahead and list the characteristics you feel off of it. Granted, the target data is somewhat irrelevant in this instance, but the feeling will still be there. I have assigned target data to these coordinates, but again, that feedback is not necessary, yet. It's more about practicing.

2014
9362

A. _____
   _____
   _____
   _____
   _____

Now, try it with the coordinates you used in the previous exercise. One at a time, write down the coordinates and immediately launch into your ideogram. Then record your "A" component. How does it feel? Did you need to probe any of the ideograms? Write everything down as it relates to the coordinates.

Still Feeling?

Are you still feeling? Good! We've gone over the "I" and the "A" components of Stage I. Now it's time for the "B." This is a tricky one, because at first glance it seems it would be easily deciphered; however, that is not always the case. The next component in working the ideogram is to state whether the target site is natural or manmade. It can only be one or the other—never both.

Like I said, it sounds simple. After all, if the target is a steel bridge, it's obviously manmade. If it's the Nile River, it's natural. But what if it's Mount Rushmore or the Sphinx? Are those manmade or natural? They are made from cliff rock, and sand, and rock, so what, then, would those qualify as? It is important that you categorize the target data correctly. A basic rule of thumb is, if it's made from nature but it's been altered to become something, it is manmade.

In order to determine if it's manmade or natural, you will put "B" directly under your "A" component and let your decision be a nondecision. Let it just come to you. If necessary, probe the ideogram again by placing your pen along the line. Once you've declared whether it's natural or manmade, you have completed most of Stage I. The CRV sheet will now look something like this.

Wanda See
7/12/14
ST: 2:47 pm
ET:

AV- yes/ popcorn and a beach, water

PI- yes/ tired, right knee hurts, missing my dog

2014
9362

A. Slow rise up, curving around,
straight down, curving under,
angle rising, arching
over, sloping down, flat,
angled down

B. Manmade

Try It Now!

I/A/B

Start again from scratch. Do not copy my example, but use the same coordinates. Get out a new piece of paper and practice by rewriting the starting information and write the coordinates again, immediately creating your ideogram. Then go ahead with the "A" and "B" components. Are any of them different than your initial trials? Are you becoming more comfortable with the process?

Now On to the "C"

The final component in Stage I is the major factor of the gestalt of the target. What is the main focus of the site? This, again, you will distinguish and record by probing the ideogram, but you have choices. In order to stay true to the remote viewing process, you must choose one of these, but I use the term "choose" lightly. As is the overall theme during Coordinate Remote Viewing, let it be a spontaneous choice. A purely reflexive selection keeps it unpolluted. Your conscious mind should be taking a back seat.

For the "C" component, your perception of the target site will either be structure, mountain, water, land, land/water interface, or life form. These are your only alternatives. A structure is obviously manmade. Then, descriptive of themselves are mountain, water, or land. Land/water interface can include such areas as shorelines, swampy areas, or even waterfalls. Life form can describe not only people but also animals or even the extreme, aliens or extraterrestrials, though I encourage you not to jump openly to that conclusion in the beginning or you will more than likely find yourself stuck.

This is one of the parts I believe is intuited. Regardless of whether you call it perceiving textures, hearing the word, or seeing the image, this is the phase where it is necessary to decode the descriptor of the target site. It's more than a guess. It's a knowing. You determine here whether the target distant in time and space is a structure, mountain, water, land, land/water interface, or life form. Once you've written it down on the paper (i.e., "C. Water" directly under the "B" component), there is no correcting it. Don't let that scare you, though. This is Stage I. There is much more to come.

Try It Now!

What It Is

Once again, put pen to paper and record your starting information. Include your name, date, start time, space for end time, and AVs or PIs. Write down the coordinates (2014, 9367), then complete your ideogram. Continue by describing the feeling or the motion of the ideogram, the "A" component. Then determine and record if the target site is natural or manmade and record that "B" component. Finally, and this may take some probing along the ideogram line, describe your perception of the main component of the gestalt as only one of the following:

Structure

Mountain

Water

Land

Land/Water Interface

Life Form

When you are all done, go back and fill in the end time, adding the words "End of Session" at the bottom of the paper with the time as well.

Was it easier to perform the functions this time? Or was it more difficult? Do your ideograms look the same or similar? What about your components? Are they different than before? Do you feel more comfortable now? Or is it confusing? Either way, there is much more to come, so get ready to move mountains! Or, at the very least, see through them!

You've already expanded your knowledge and worked with Coordinate Remote Viewing through the exercises you've done. During the practicing you may have noticed you needed to take a break on occasion, or you were feeling like you were already receiving impressions about target data because your mind was wandering as you were working. As you continue performing the exercises, you will find you absolutely need to take breaks. Not to worry! This is normal, and it is a very significant part of Coordinate Remote Viewing. So much so that taking a break requires you to name what kind of break you are taking. The next chapter will teach you how to figure that out.

"Once in a while you have to take a break and visit yourself."
—Audrey Giorgi

Chapter Eight
Breaks

Get Out of Your Own Way

If you've made it this far in the book, you believe in the possibility that we have the power to transcend time and space and gather information. So what then holds us back from being great? What stops us from consistently being successful with our remote viewing sessions? That's actually a complicated question with a pretty simplistic answer: Get out of your own head! That's right, stop analyzing with your conscious mind! Then, and only then, will you begin to have really good and pleasurable experiences. Letting go of your ego, self-doubt, and worry is the only way to truly begin reaping the benefits of remote viewing.

As with psychic sight, CRV depends upon having the capacity to not only quiet the inner dialogue but also to let go of the outcome. Moving forward without concern about whether you are right or wrong does not mean that when you are done you can't receive feedback or validation. It's quite the opposite. Feedback helps you learn and teaches you what you are doing right and if you are doing anything wrong. No one person, and I repeat, no one person will ever be one hundred percent accurate with remote viewing, whether it is psychic or coordinate. If you are hoping to be that one person, forget it. It won't happen. Striving for that perfection is fine, but give yourself a break! Putting pressure on yourself to be the best can hinder, or even stop, your progress. Remember to let go of your ego for better results.

Analytical Overlay (AOL)

One of the ways to remove your own ego and imagination from the session is to declare any analytical, intellectual, or even psychic beliefs you attach to the target data. It is an extremely simple process but one that carries with it great importance. If not done, it can hinder the entire session and cause a false viewing, making it harder to tune in to the real signal line data.

Declaring an analytical overlay, or AOL, is easy. But what exactly does that mean? Thinking you've deciphered your target data right off the bat, or even as you progress through the stages, is very common and more destructive to the outcome than you might imagine. The human mind is very analytical. It wants to name what it is you're seeing. It tries, at every turn, to put things together neatly so they can be categorized, qualified, and quantified. Normally, this is not an issue. However, with CRV it can be a huge deterrent to locking onto the target.

During one of my training sessions with remote viewing, I was assigned a coordinate and was doing great. I'd connected to the signal line and was receiving what I perceived to be substantial and worthy data. I assumed I was on the right path. Then I saw an image, which I proceeded to draw on my paper. The only way to describe it is to say it looked like a football. It was that shape. This immediately began a train of thoughts in my mind of playing football, football stadiums, NFL, youth football, cheerleaders, etc. The problem with that was it wasn't a football. Luckily, I declared an AOL and wrote "football" so I was able to let it go. Otherwise I may have held on to that belief of it being a football rather than continuing to receive more input about the target data. Recording and declaring the conclusion your mind has jumped to allows the thoughts of those images to float away, leaving you free to resume gathering data on your target site. It is possible, of course, that the information you believe to be an AOL is actual target data, but this is very rare. Usually it's just your mind lending a reference point to the information you are getting, so you don't want to confuse that with the actual target coordinates. In this particular instance, when I declared an AOL break and wrote "football," the target site was actually the Hindenburg. The shape of my analytical overlay made perfect sense. Luckily I was able to recognize it and declare it, allowing me to release the thought of it being a football.

Analytical overlay will more often than not disrupt the signal line, causing a shift in what you're viewing or connecting to. This not only makes the data that you are collecting incorrect, but it also disrupts the purity of the actual target site, making it harder to view. By declaring a break you allow the signal line to be put on hold while you eject the AOL. This is one of the most common types of breaks, but there are more coming up that are designed to also help expel any distractions.

When the AOL continues to come into the session, and is now driving it, more time is needed to dispel the analytical overlay and an AOL Drive Break is required. When you are no longer able to produce viable data, and instead are manufacturing spurious information based on your AOL, it's break time. You are no longer objective.

Try It Now!

Sampling Analytical Overlay

Imagine hearing the following description of a target site—either as someone is explaining it to you, or as the impressions you receive during a session. Do you draw any conclusions before you find out what the target is? Have you decided you know exactly where you are? Does it sound familiar to you? Do you recognize it? What do you think the target is?

"I am looking at the target site. I see what looks like a large rectangle shape stretching out ahead of me. It appears it may have water in it, surrounded by flat area. It's a place lots of people come to congregate and it seems to be some kind of destination, possibly vacation. It is

outside and the sun is shining. Ahead, at the end, it looks like there may be multistory decks overlooking this rectangle. There are curved and pointed objects reaching up toward the sky. There is walking space next to it, people are there and there are structures on either side—possibly pools, walls, benches, or even seats. Moving to the left and down at ground level, there are multiple levels to this target; I see a mammoth white structure surrounded by blue water. This target object is hundreds of feet long, and has multiple spires or smoke stacks sticking up off the top of the structure, either rounded or curved, as well as straight. There are a lot of windows in a row, lined up. There are railings all around it and people are standing behind the railings looking out. I can see gold and white, opulence. People come inside and on the deck of this place. Backing up away from the object further I can now see a palm tree on the shoreline. It is a manmade structure, very rich looking."

Write down any thoughts you may have about the target data. Do you think you know what it is? Does it sound like something you may know or recognize? Write down what you think it may be, using great detail. Remember, the object of this exercise is to actually try and decipher, using the description of the target, what you think it may be. Most people will form a preconceived idea basing their opinion in the data provided.

There were many descriptive words provided. Go back and reread the paragraph. Does it become clearer? More confusing? If you correctly guessed, you're amazing! (I never would have gotten it!) If not, no worries. This is a very tough one!

Target Feedback Data

The target is the Crystal Mosque, located at 21000 Kuala Terengganu, Terengganu, Malaysia. Most people guess the target is a cruise ship. Take a moment to look up images of the Crystal Mosque and cruise ship pictures on the Internet. You will see there are many similarities. Enough, in fact, to make you feel almost like it is the same place when comparing the pictures to each other. Pay special attention to how similar they appear from specific directions and angles.

It is very natural to jump to a conclusion about what it is you are viewing. When you compare different images of the Crystal Mosque with various cruise ship pictures it becomes even more obvious how easy it is to do. I've noticed, as well, that anyone who also works with their psychic vision or clairvoyance tends to see more images that can interrupt or confuse the target data, creating the need to take an AOL Break.

How to Record Breaks

Declaring a break is easy. The hardest part is realizing you have experienced an AOL. Once you've determined this has occurred, you simply write on the far right of your paper "AOL Break—Cruise Ship," or something along those lines. This allows the guessing to be put to rest, letting the signal line be tapped back into. If, however, you've decided you are experiencing AOL Drive, you'd need to declare an AOL Drive Break, record what the AOL is, and then take an extra step. You need to stop your session by writing AOL Drive Break. This allows you to walk away and take a real break.

Once you've had enough time to relax a bit, you can pick the session back up. To do this, simply write "Resume Session" with the time. Much of CRV is about intent. Your intent is to connect with something distant in time and space. By recording the AOL Break and Resume Session, you are setting your intention and sending to the signal line that it is time to begin again. In essence you are ready to refocus your intention to connect to the matrix and begin receiving information again.

Using the same example as above, it would look something like this:

Wanda See
7/12/14
ST: 2:47 pm
ET:

AV- yes/ popcorn and a beach, water

PI- yes/ tired, right knee hurts, missing my dog

2014
9362

Slow rise up, curving around, straight
down, curving under, angle rising, arching
over, sloping down, flat, angled down

B. Manmade

C. Structure

AOL Drive Break
Cruise ship—vacation cruise ship

Resume Session 3:15

Other Breaks

An AOL Break is not the only break to expect. There are other breaks to be utilized when necessary. A **Confusion Break** is used when the viewer can't help mixing up the surroundings he's in with the target data. The impressions received are meshed together with the physical and mental stimuli present in the viewer's environment. A **Too Much Break** (**TM Break**) is used when the viewer is overwhelmed by all of the information coming in from the signal line and needs to slow it down. This is apparent especially when multiple ideograms are produced or the ideogram is incredibly elaborate. An **Personal Inclemency Break** (**PI Break**) is necessary when the viewer is overcome by some type of distress or inclemency such as what was declared in the beginning of the session. For example, if the viewer has a headache that's gotten worse, and can't function, it's considered time for a Personal Inclemency Break. If, after the viewer receives the coordinates, an ideogram can't be produced, a **Missed Break** is declared. This allows the viewer to try again to connect to the signal line.

A **Bi-location Break** (**BI Break**) is needed if the viewer becomes too absorbed in their target site and cannot objectively report back information. This also occurs if the viewer cannot move past the remote viewing room. An **Emotional Impact Break** (**EI Break**) occurs when the viewer becomes overwhelmed with an emotion such as grief, hysteria, fear, etc. A break must be declared in order to objectify and release the emotion that seems to be attached to the target site. An **Aesthetic Impact Break** is declared if the site has impressed upon you a feeling. For example, feeling happy to be there or sad. Also, this break is necessary when there is a feeling of "Holy Cow! This target is huge!" or "Wow, this is really gross!"

Finally, if at any time a break is necessary and cannot be deemed one of the above, no worries. Just declare a **Break**, and **Resume** when you're ready! Now that you know you are able to slow it down if needed, you are fully prepared to move on to Stage II and begin describing what it is you are targeting.

"Lose your mind and come to your senses."
—Frederick Salomon Perls

Chapter Nine

Stage II

Using Your Senses

Everything you've always known, you have learned through your senses. This is exactly what happens in Coordinate Remote Viewing Stage II; it's all about your senses. Once you've dropped into the target site, having done your ideogram work, it's time for the next stage.

One-word descriptors are what are needed here. Any senses you have when you physically walk into a place are the same senses we are looking for in CRV. You want to write down everything you sense about the target data, using basic words. The correct format for this is to record what you receive down the center of the page and to write <u>S II</u> (for Stage II) above it as the header. For example, if target coordinates brought you to a busy beach, your page may look something like this:

S II
Bright
Sandy
Salty
Ocean smell
Laughter

Noisy

Blue

Tan

Brown

Green

Multicolored

White

Hot

Warm

Breezy

Soft

Wet

Squishy

Gritty

These are basic sense words, or sensory words. These include sounds, sights, smells, tastes, and tactile impressions. If the descriptions go beyond basic words they become unreliable and more subjective then objective.

Try It Now!

Working with Sense

Without going through all of the steps of Stage I, you are going to jump right into Stage II, with one major difference—you will know what your target is! This is a form of frontloading: supplying the viewer with information before they jump in. In this instance, it's perfect and will help you to practice.

Grab a pen and a piece of paper. Go somewhere peaceful and have a seat where you won't be disturbed during this exercise. You will be writing, so make sure you've gone somewhere you can do that comfortably. Put your pen to paper and get ready to write. Take a nice deep breath to try and clear your head. Take another deep breath and focus on a beautiful white light emanating around you, giving you energy to connect to the signal line and the matrix. Take another deep breath, and another, until you feel totally relaxed.

When you are ready, write your name. Then write down "Living Room" in the middle of your page. Now, down the center, write down all of the sensory or descriptive words you can about your living room. If you don't have a living room, use the room where you are most often, such as family room, den, etc. Just when you think you've written enough, write down a few more. Remember, these are things you receive or perceive only as you would through sensory input: sight, smell, taste, sound, and touch. Do not include any emotions or feelings you have about the living room. This is not the place you'd write down "love" or "fun" or "boring." Record colors and other descriptors here.

Now, review your list. Is there anything on the list of words you've written that you couldn't physically smell, see, taste, touch, or hear? If so, it should not be on there. Cross it off. After you've done that, review your list again. Do all of the words you've recorded make sense? Do they fit with your living room?

Count the number of words you've written down. Though quality is important for CRV, so is quantity. You want to include as much information about the target site as possible. Do you have at least ten words? If so, great! You're catching on! Do you have more than twenty? Awesome! You're really getting the hang of it! If you have more than thirty, pat yourself on the back! You did amazingly well!

Dimensionals

Just as in the physical world, target sites have dimension. This means they can be described using single words pertaining to three-dimensional objects. As you progress through Stage II, you may find you need to see more or less of your target. This can be accomplished in a couple of ways. The first way is to adjust the *aperture*, or the amount of information you are receiving from the signal line. Similar to a camera lens taking photographs, we can adjust our aperture to open wider and view more of the target, or close down a bit to get a more focused or detailed image. What you are trying to view in CRV is the gestalt, or the heart, of the person, place, thing, or event, and fine-tuning the aperture can help pinpoint what you need to be viewing.

Basic dimensionals may include height, width, depth, and size. As you can imagine, if you were viewing the Empire State Building, you would want the aperture open wide to get the full dimensions. Otherwise, you may only see a reflection of a window or the gray of the metal and concrete structure. You can also recall any energetics here, or energy words. Bouncing, pulsing, and shaking are all forms of energetics. When recording dimensional data, you are still in Stage II and would write your words under your sensory data in a column down the center of the page. For example, if the target data were a lighthouse, you might see this for Stage II dimensionals:

S II
Large
Tall
Thin
Vertical
Hollow
Round
Pointy
Buzzing
Pulsing

Try It Now!

Gathering Dimensions

It's your turn. Get your pen and paper and get comfy. Just as you did for the sensing part of Stage II, it's time to practice your dimensionals. Breathe deeply and close your eyes for a moment. Imagine first whether you are in a wealthy community, an average-income community, or a poorer community. Then, imagine being at the community pool. Feel as if you are transported there, able to look all around the area. Next, begin recording any Stage II data you can. Be sure to include sizes, shapes, etc. that are present and any energetics that you perceive. Remember, this list goes down the center of the page.

When you are finished, go back over what you've written. Does it make sense? Does anything not belong here? Were you able to get at least three dimensionals and one energetic? Great! How about five dimensionals and two energetics? If so, awesome! If not, no worries. You are still practicing. If you got as many as ten dimensionals and three energetics, that is a lot! Give yourself a hand—you've come a long way!

Working with Sketches

While in Stage II, you may also begin to receive images. It is during this stage that you are able to draw simple line sketches. These would be drawn in the left third of the page. These are not meant to be complicated drawings, just basic representations of the image you are seeing or thinking while in the matrix.

After you draw the picture, probe it like you did the ideogram and write descriptions as you go. For example, if you drew what looked like a box, you may have an AOL of a box. So you would, of course, write that on the right-hand side. But as you're probing it you may sense "wood," and "asphalt," and "vinyl." This may invoke a new AOL, of a house. Again, you would record that. Quite often, as with psychic sight or clairvoyance, we receive symbols that are meant to represent something else. The symbols are just easier to decipher than the actual object is.

These sketches may then invoke more Stage II descriptors, including sensory data, dimensionals, and energetics. When that happens, Stage II should be continued.

"For me, drawing generates thinking and vice versa."
—Helmut Jahn

Chapter Ten
Stage III

Sometimes it's challenging to know when to move into Coordinate Remote Viewing Stage III. One of the best ways to determine if you're ready to move on is to adjust the aperture wide. If you immediately become inundated with target information, then it's time to continue forward into this stage. If information is halted or still coming through in little bits and pieces, you need to focus still on Stage II. Stage III is when you begin playing in the big time, so to speak. You are going to get more information and more data, and images will become clearer than they were in the first two stages. Now you need to be open to adjusting your vision.

Another way to change what you are seeing, along with adjusting your aperture, is to move within the site. Depending upon the coordinates, the viewer is able to go dirctly to that point in space and time and tap into the signal line, to retrieve the data from the target site that is relevant or that needs decoding. Sometimes in order to do this we need to adjust our location, or our aspect ratio, or vantage point.

There are two different ideas of the concept of movement, and it's important to recognize the difference. Motion at the site is when people or objects are actually moving in the target site. Imagine your target is a track meet at the local college. When you're viewing this event you may see the competitors running or the spectators cheering. This is a motion at the actual target. Separate and different from this motion is actually shifting your perspective of the site, or mobility. Mobility is important in CRV because it's through this that we are able to change our awareness of the target site and see it from a new direction. If we are viewing a beach and all we see is a vast body of water, we won't get any other details. Moving our perspective—turning around, for instance—can provide us with the people at the beach, a concession stand, a parking lot, an amusement park, etc. There is so much more to be gained from simply changing your viewpoint.

Change the cueing bracket (i.e., [Move 100' up]) by moving closer, farther away, up, down, to the right, to the left, and then do it again if necessary. With every move more data is gathered. The idea is that this will make known all perspectives of the target site, which can be extremely important in gathering substantial data, but even more so in being accurate with the information you are gaining.

Move It

When I was targeting the Statue of Liberty, I was stuck in the basement. All I could see were tunnels and a star shape. At the time, I didn't know I was in the base of the statue; I simply thought that was my target. Then I began moving. I moved up one hundred feet. I was able to see a staircase and a lot of metal, but I still didn't have a great vantage point, though again, I didn't know that yet. Then I moved two hundred feet outward, making sure to land outside the target. This was where I needed to be to see the distinguishing features of the pleating of the gown, the hand up in the air holding the torch, the face, and even the grass outside and around it. I drew my sketch to reflect this. I immediately had an AOL of a large woman, somewhere hot, possibly Africa, swatting flies. I knew I had to declare that right away!

You can also change how you view your target data by changing the time of day. Imagine being dropped into a site, especially outside, when it is pitch black. It will be very difficult to see. You can ask to change to a time when you have daylight with which to view the target data better, or even ask that it be illuminated so you may see it better. But remember, depending on the coordinates, changing the time of day or even the date may not always serve you well, especially if you're looking for a specific event or to see if a person or object is present in the location you are viewing.

Try It Now!

Shifting Focus

Dropping down into a target can afford you a wonderful view if you land in the right place. For this exercise, you are going to land in the wrong place and need to move. It will be up to you to decide how and where to move. You have an advantage over a regular CRV session, though. You will know what the target is, so it will be easier to adjust your vantage point.

Take a nice deep breath. Now, imagine your target is a local department store. Let's make it Sears, if you have one you'd recognize. Sears carries everything from tools to bedding to clothing to appliances to televisions, and then some. But you are not landing in the middle of Sears during a busy shopping day. Instead, you are landing in the target site in the dressing room at 1:00 a.m. Immediately, what you'll see and feel is a tiny room, especially if there are full-length doors containing the small space. It will be extremely dark and probably feel a bit cramped and confining.

But your challenge is to figure out how you will determine where you are. Will you move? Will you illuminate the space? Will you change the time of day? Will you move up? Down? North? South? What steps would you take to view the target data better?

Remember, if you go too large or move too high you may end up viewing the whole mall as the target site. If you move down too far you may end up in the bowels of the space underneath the mall, and who knows what is down there!

Did it feel good to move? Did you choose to change the time of day or illuminate the space first before you moved anywhere?

How did you know what to do or where to move? Did you make a mistake and end up too far out, or too far down, or too far up? Were you able to fix that by moving your vantage point yet again?

You can practice this anywhere with any target you can imagine. Just be careful—you don't want to play in traffic!

Drawing the Target Data Out

In Stage II you began to sketch objects or items you've come across during your viewing if they happened to pop up, and you've probed them for information. Stage III takes that a bit further by encouraging the drawings and making them center stage. Instead of the drawings being a result of the Stage II data you are recording, the sensory data, and basic dimensionals, they are now the main focus in Stage III.

With every simple sketch, you are focusing in on the dimensions of the target data.

The basic premise behind the sketches is to have something more concrete, more developed, to probe. Acquiring the target data without sketches would leave so much out that it would not give the viewer, or the monitor or whoever contracted the viewing, a complete picture of the site. Probing and labeling the contour sketches then becomes the priority after each drawing is done in order to provide more detailed data on the target site.

Using the Crystal Mosque as our example, after you've moved all the way up and begun Stage III your page might look something like this:

Wanda See
7/12/14
ST: 2:47 pm
ET:

AV- yes/ popcorn and a beach, water

PI- yes/ tired, right knee hurts, missing my dog

2014
9362 ~~~

*A. Slow rise up, curving around, straight
down, curving under, angle rising, arching
over, sloping down, flat, angled down*

B. Manmade

C. Structure

AOL Drive Break
Cruise ship-vacation cruise ship

Resume Session

S II   ②

White
Gold
Gray
Blue
Warm
Hot
Ocean scent
Salt scent
Voices
Smooth
Round
Sharp
Spicy
Reflective
Tropical
Wet
Buttery taste
Salty taste

AOL Popcorn

③

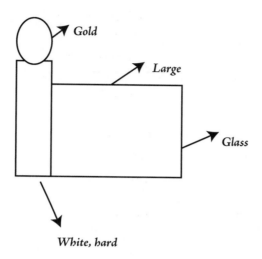

Gold

Large

Glass

White, hard

AOL Building

Large
Deep
Buzzing energy
Shiny
Breezy

AI Break
Wow-this is really big!

[Move up 200']

④

S III

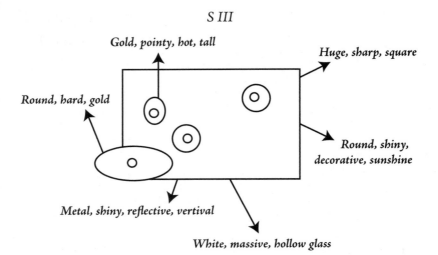

Gold, pointy, hot, tall

Huge, sharp, square

Round, hard, gold

Round, shiny,
decorative, sunshine

Metal, shiny, reflective, vertival

White, massive, hollow glass

**AOL Building with
gold onion domes on top**

**AI Break
I feel really overwhelmed and in awe**

Resume

[Move 50' to the left]

⑤

[Move down 100']

Huge, white, concrete, metal, square, tall, volumous, horizontal

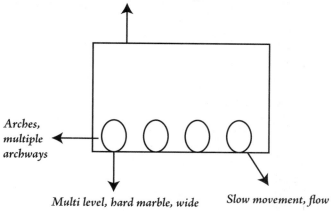

Arches,
multiple
archways

Multi level, hard marble, wide   *Slow movement, flow*

AOL People walking

Notice how in Stage II,I the drawings have given you a new depth into the target. They become more important, are probed more deeply, and more descriptions are present. The dimensionals have a greater impact on the target site. There is mobility or movement around the target site to get better, more detailed data. There is also energy present of *Slow movement and Flow.*

Declare It

During this stage many people begin to feel sensitive to the coordinates. Simply put, it may make them feel yucky. It can also cause them to feel elated, or scared, or excited. They may also feel like the target is gross, or disgusting, or even heinous. These are all examples of AI, and it's extremely important, especially as you move through Stage III, to declare these emotions, thoughts, and feelings, and allow them to dissipate totally. If they aren't entirely gone from the viewer, they can, and most definitely will, taint the remainder of the viewing session.

AIs (Aesthetic Impacts) and AOLs (Analytical Overlays) are not always a bad thing. Sometimes what you are getting as an AI or an AOL is exactly spot-on. You are picking up the target site from the signal line with incredible accuracy. But that is not what is important here in this moment. What's important with CRV is that you gather all of the evidence and the data you possibly can about the coordinates and hold off summarizing what you think it may be until the very end.

The more practice a remote viewer has, the more they will understand when they are ready to jump from one stage of the process to the next. It is not based on time spent; it's more about the information that is coming through the signal line. When the aperture is opened wider and the data is spilling in, it's time to draw.

Try It Now!

Where You Live

Again, no worries, because you are not going to be graded on this exercise! This is not an exam, nor is it even a blind target! Get comfortable. Be somewhere with a lot of paper and a pen where you won't be disturbed for a bit. Now, close your eyes and relax. Take a few deep breaths.

Imagine you are given the coordinates for your home, and you've dropped into the site and are viewing it from up in the sky looking down. Draw and label whatever images you receive from that site. Do not get up and look outside; just draw whatever images and shapes come to mind. Label them using all of the sensory, dimensional, and energetic data you receive from the signal line. Be sure to include any AIs you may have. You already know what the target is, so chances are you won't have any additional AOLs, but if you do, go ahead and record them.

Then move. Move yourself by using the brackets and write [Move north 50']. Now where are you? Draw whatever images you receive and label them. You are obviously very familiar with where you live, but chances are you haven't analyzed it this closely. There may be data you don't recognize or didn't remember, or maybe don't expect. Draw it and label it.

Then move again. [Move east 75']. Draw whatever you see. Again, don't forget to include any AIs you may have as well as AOLs. You may find a bird's nest, or even a bees' nest that you weren't expecting. If so, great, though I hope you don't get stung trying to remove a bees' nest!

When you are all done with that drawing, move again. This time in whatever direction you prefer. If you need to illuminate the target site or change the time of day, do that as well. Is there any movement within the site? Note that. Are there any energetics that need to be recorded? Feel free to move a few more times. Depending on the size and dimensions of your home, you may have quite a bit to view!

When you are all done, go over your drawings and how you labeled them. Do they look right to you? Does it appear you've labeled everything from memory or were you at the target site? When you are all done, go outside and compare your sketches with the real thing. (Don't fall off the roof, though!) Do they match up? Are there differences? Did it feel comfortable to draw and label everything? Or did you feel like you were grasping for information?

No matter how it felt, give yourself credit. You were able to put pen to paper and actually do the exercise. You are one step closer to being a remote viewer!

Congratulations!

You are one of the few choice people who have made it through the first three stages of Coordinate Remote Viewing. Congratulate yourself! With practice, the sky is the limit. You can actually run with it and be confident that what you've done up until now has given you the direction and the tools to move forward to begin seeing people, places, or events distant in space and time in the way the government and the scientists who created the process intended. Coordinate Remote Viewing is at your fingertips now; you just need to grab on and become one with the procedure. Reviewing and doing all of the previous exercises again will help you with everything you've learned up to this point. It will also afford you the opportunity to increase your skill level at tuning in to the signal line to gather data from your target.

Completing Stages I, II, and III (and adding the summary session described on page 161, "It's A Wrap") allows you to begin performing CRV sessions. However, following through and completing the remaining stages will help you gain more knowledge and wisdom, and create a more in-depth environment that will increase the information you will be able to process through remote viewing. The more you know, the better you will be. So although you can easily stop here, you will get better as you move forward. Enjoy the next phase of Coordinate Remote Viewing!

"Unfortunately, no one can be told what the Matrix is.
You have to see it for yourself."

—Morpheus, from the movie *The Matrix*

Chapter Eleven

Stage IV and Stage V

You've come to a crossroads now. You can either continue on and finish the CRV process, or you can just practice the first three stages. It's entirely up to you. Coordinate Remote Viewing can definitely be accomplished with what you've already learned as long as you wrap it up at the end. But to really get in there and expand the target data you receive, you need to complete the remaining stages of the process.

Stage IV

In a way, Stage IV is like a summary, though it's not the same as the summary at the end. Think of it as a way to get all your ducks in a row. This section works by separating, but putting together the various aspects of, all the work you've done before and adding new data to that. Sensory data, dimensionals, aesthetic impacts, emotional impacts, and analytic overlays are all recorded using a table sort of format. In addition to the descriptors already explored, Tangibles, Intangibles, and Analytical Overlay Signal are also now introduced.

Tangibles are objects or things you can actually touch. So, as a viewer these would be things like furniture, buildings, cars, or trees. Tangibles

147

are also things that you can't actually touch but are present, such as smells and temperature. Intangibles are more like ideas or functions. For instance, the concept of administration or planning would be considered intangible. Likewise, medical, religious, governmental, etc., are all intangibles. These are things that cannot be physically touched. Finally, Analytical Overlay Signal (AOL/S) is about looking through the AOL without declaring a break because it represents the actual target. During a CRV session, seeing an image of the New England Patriots' Gillette Stadium when the real target is the Dallas Cowboys' AT&T Stadium would be an example of an AOL/S.

Understanding the Matrix

Now that you know what goes into this next stage, it's time to put it in the correct format. Remember, everything you do in CRV has a specific order—Stage IV is no different. In fact, this stage is known as the matrix and begins with column headings as below.

S2	D	A	EI	T	I	AOL	AOL/S
___	___	___	___	___	___	___	___
Sensory	Dimensionals	Aesthetic Impact	Emotional Impact	Tangibles	Intangibles	AOL	AOL/Signal

Just because you've already worked with some of these heading categories doesn't mean you should use what you have already recorded. The point to this section is to tune in to the signal line and pick up anything that comes in now. It may be the same information, but hopefully you will get more and better detailed data to add to what you've already written down.

Again, it's about format. So the process of this stage is to record the data that comes through for you in a staggered diagonal line. Simply stated, you will begin with sensory data, listing anything you pick up in the column underneath "S2." Then, when you are done with all of the S2 data you have, you will move on to the dimensionals and write them down in the same column format under the "D" heading. When you look back at the page, it will look as though the words are flowing downward in a slanted fashion. As with the rest of the process, this may take up multiple pages, so allow for that possibility.

If you use the local grocery store parking lot as the coordinates, you may find Stage IV looking something like the Stage IV Matrix chart on the next pages.

So, using that much-abbreviated example, you can see that the matrix for Stage IV can be very helpful in putting everything all together. It is also valuable in categorizing the data from the signal line into usable details that will help to summarize and understand the target site. In addition, you can sketch and label drawings during this process just as you did through the previous stages.

Try It Now!

Putting It All On the Table

Set yourself somewhere comfortable with pen and plenty of paper. Be sure you understand what is expected from you for each of the column headings in Stage IV. You are going to be asked to follow Stage IV protocol and write down whatever information you receive about your target, but you want a clear and precise idea of just what you need to record before you start.

When you are sure you comprehend each category, write them down across your paper. Then, get ready to tune in to your coordinates by closing your eyes and taking a few deep breaths to relax your mind, body, and spirit.

Now, put your pen to the paper in the column under "S2" so you can begin. Your coordinates are the local hospital. Start tuning in to the signal line and write down all of your sensory information. Before you move onto the next section, make sure you've exhausted every single "S2" item you can. Do this with all of the columns.

S2	D	AI	EI
Hot			
Multicolor			
Black			
Horn			
Breezy			
Exhaust smell			
Talking sound			
Green			
White			
Yellow			
Food smell			
	Wide		
	Expansive		
	Flat		
	Bumpy		
		Tired	
		Stressed	
		Hungry	
			None

T	I	AOL	AOL/S
Metal			
Pavement			
Cars			
Yellow lines			
Trees			
Grass			
Bushes			
Building			
	Shopping		
	Cooking		
	Eating		
		Cars	
		People	
		Mall	
		Restaurant	
			Used car lot

When you are all done, look over your data. If you were reading it, would you know exactly where you were? If someone else were to read it would they know where they were? Is it easily recognizable as a hospital? Can you clearly distinguish this particular hospital from another one? For something generic like this, it may be more difficult and the AOL Signal line may never match up exactly to the specific location, but you never know! Stranger things have happened!

Stage V

This stage is interesting. It takes you a step beyond and requires you to analyze information that has been building up to this point. All of the information you've been accessing through the signal line has imprinted on your psyche and is there to be recalled. This section is about your interpretation of the data you have accumulated. In order to execute this phase, it is critical to be mindful of the possibility of AOLs. By separating the information into four different categories, your focus shifts and allows you to express data for each of the following: Objects, Attributes, Subject, and Topics.

Referred to as *cognitrons*, groups of neurons have come together to form an idea or concept and can be induced to service by prompting. By taking each category one at a time and listing the various attributes that come to mind, you can open up the target site. As usual, there is a strict procedure to be followed to avoid any contaminating AOLs, or even imagination, coming to the surface instead of the pertinent information.

First come the Objects. Take, for example, the concept of medicine. If you were remote viewing coordinates and you came up with the concept of medicine during the session, this would be one of the Stage V items you could further explore. You would begin by writing "medical" down, with "objects" underneath it, forming a column again. Under that, and to get the ball rolling, you would write "emanations?" By writing emanations and placing a question mark after it, you are calling on your subconscious mind to pull up and emit any objects that made or make you think of medicine. Objects are things or people you can actually touch. So it may look like this:

Medical
Objects
Emanations?

Pills
Hospital
Sick people
Needles
Stethoscope
Machines
Beds
Robes
Operating lights
IV bags

Along the same vein as Stage IV, the columns continue in a staggered diagonal fashion down the page. After Objects comes Attributes. An attribute is a quality or characteristic of a thing or a person or even a place. So, following suit, it would look something like this:

Medical
Attributes
Emanations?

Cold
Warm
Large
Expansive
Hollow
Busy
Loud
Quiet

After writing down everything that has come up from your subconscious for Objects and Attributes, it's time to move on to Subjects. A subject is something that is discussed, or the purpose or nature of something. It is the function of, or activities of, what it is you're discovering. It would look something like this:

Medical

Subjects

Emanations?

Heal

Operate

Help

Fix

Comfort

Learn

Teach

Finally, when you have provided all the information you can by addressing the first three categories, you will tap into the topic of the data you are bringing forth. Remember, this is not taken from the signal line or even the matrix. Rather, it's similar to accessing information from a computer storage device. You've already recorded it in memory; you're just recalling it to develop the target site further.

Topics is kind of a tough one in that it is very similar to the others, specifically Subjects and Attributes. Topics are typically the subject of a discussion. Quite often this category becomes almost a subcategory of one or more of the Subjects you've already recalled. In the above example, it may look something like this:

Medical
Topics
Emanations?

Doctor
Medicine/
Drugs
Protocol
Aging
Disease
Nurse
Religion
Healer

Coming to a conclusion that the target site is relevant in a particular way is easy given all of the different steps of discovery. You may find as you move through this stage that there are overlapping ideas in the categories as well as in each cognitron. Imagine the different concepts you may come up with during a CRV session. If you are viewing a hospital, for example, you may come up with medical, or religious, or administrative, or teaching, which can all be broken down in Stage V. You want to address and break out as many cognitrons as possible to provide a fuller description of the target site.

Try It Now!

Memories

As always, go somewhere you can be relaxed and comfortable with pen and paper. Take a few deep breaths and write "Stage V" on the top of your paper. You are going to dig into your memories to pull out information for the four categories: Objects, Attributes, Subjects, and Topics. Your cognitron is "Religious." Start by creating your first column like this:

Religious
Objects
Emanations?

Once your pen hits the paper and you finish the question mark, it should trigger any object data to rise from your subconscious mind and flow through to your page. When you've written everything that comes up for a specific category, it's time to move to the next column.

Look over the data you've recorded. Does it all make sense? Have you inserted the information into the correct categories? Does anything need to be changed? How did it feel to do this exercise? Was it easy? Difficult? Were one or more of the categories harder to fill in than the others?

Possible Contamination

During Stage V you may find yourself listing descriptors in the wrong categories. Sometimes this occurs because you are ready to move on to the next one but just haven't physically changed where you are writing. Other times it occurs because there's just no information for that particular category. This is okay. Just take note and move on.

Another form of possible contamination of the process is using AOLs or AOL/Ss as your cognitron. A cognitron, again, is basically a word used to summarize a group or a cluster of elements that make up a concept. You can think of it as a kind of storage device that can be accessed. This concept, if it is based on an analytical overlay, can pollute the whole process if it's not recognized. This is all right to do, though, as long as you are aware it is possibly a mere AOL and not the actual target. However, this often will happen to help you break down each cognitron, and may in fact expose the real target data through the process.

"Change the way you see things,
and the things you see will change."

—Wayne Dyer

Chapter Twelve

Stage VI

Building It

You will start this final stage of Coordinate Remote Viewing by using the same type of matrix you created in Stage IV. In addition, it's time to construct a model. Now, having said that, that does not mean you will specifically be making an exact replica of your target site. Rather, the coordinates you are viewing will be explored further during this stage. Creating the model will help you to receive more details about the target data from the signal line.

It's time to get your hands dirty! Throughout this whole CRV process you've been very busy writing. This is not going to stop, but you will now add to that by creating a 3D object of the target site! Tuning in to the target data using your kinesthetic senses will help to truly decode it.

Try It Now!

Making Your Model

Using clay or Play-Doh, make a model of the outside of your neighbor's house. It doesn't have to be perfect, but do it from inside your own home without looking outside. As you add the details, think about what you are doing and what information comes to mind. Does it feel like you gain more knowledge of the feeling of the house or what happens inside the home? Do you feel the temperature or the colors? Are the lives of the people living there impressed upon you as you are working?

Think about the data you've collected. Does it make sense based on what you know? Do you feel like you've received information you didn't know of before?

Mix it up a bit after that. Focus your thoughts on the kitchen. Does that change the way you mold your clay? What about if you shift to the bedroom area? Does it make you feel emotional in any way? Does your modeling change even though you are still building the outside of the home? Notice all of the information you have received. Does it change the way you view your neighbors?

Why You Build

The main point to this stage is not the actual rendering of the model, but instead, the information gained while building the model. Using clay, the most common medium, you are kinesthetically opening yourself to gathering additional knowledge from the signal line that you may or may not have been privy to before. As the model is being constructed, the idea is to objectify anything that comes to mind and write it down on the new matrix. The information may begin slowing down as the modeling starts building up, but the representation of data is still there.

The matrix in this stage may end up looking different than the matrix in Stage V. Previously the matrix was filled in on the diagonal, moving from one category to the next. That meant that in order to follow procedure, you would record all of the "S2" data first, then move on to the dimensionals, and complete the matrix that way. This Stage VI matrix is different in that the format or structure is not based on the necessity to complete one aspect before beginning the next. Instead, you will record the information as it comes while working on creating the model. If you use a local movie theater showing a scary movie as the target, the matrix may look something like this:

Stage 6 Matrix Chart

S-2	D	Al	El	T	I	AOL	AOL/S
Dark							
	Voluminous	Sleepy					
			Scared, Nervous	Material			
					Acting		
	Loud					Stage, Movie	
				Speakers			
					Vision		
						Freddy Kreuger	Theater
							Movie
							Theater

Logical or Illogical?

This is a very fascinating concept: that the matrix will be different depending upon which stage you are in. It's interesting because you may find you enjoy or feel more comfortable recording information in one way versus the other. This usually is because we learn to function in our everyday lives a certain way.

They say a messy desk is a sign of an intelligent mind. I'm glad! That's me all the way. If everything is too ordered I feel stifled. I don't know if that's a function of my creativity, or intuition, or just who I naturally am. I need to have five different things going on around me or I can't focus. Others cringe at the thought that their desk is not perfectly organized and crave organization in order to survive in society.

I find that I prefer the Stage VI matrix to Stage V because it seems somewhat chaotic and I don't feel as limited, though the Stage V matrix definitely has its merits—it challenges us to pull a steady stream of intel from the signal line, and makes it essential that we gather up all of the knowledge we possibly can, one category at a time. On the other hand, the Stage VI matrix seems to be more how my mind works, with thoughts and data popping in from every direction—still connected to the signal line, but allowing my brain to constantly move.

Try It Now!

Visit the Movies with Coordinates

With your supplies, go somewhere comfortable and be ready to write. Using your local movie theater coordinates as the target, create a Stage V matrix. When you've finished recording all you can, put down your pen and turn over those papers that you wrote on.

Next, pick up a fresh sheet and your pen and create a Stage VI matrix, again using your local theater as the coordinates. After you're done, again put down your pen and turn your sheet(s) over.

Without looking at what you have written down, think about which was easier. Which felt better to you? Did either flow more smoothly? Did it feel like you were pulling teeth to gain insight into the target for either method?

Now, look at the pages. Which has more information? Is one more detailed than the other? Count the number of actual descriptors on the pages and compare. Does one have more than the other? Compare this against which one felt better to actually do. Does it make sense? Does it seem to be in line with what you thought? Or are you surprised?

Remember, preparing the matrixes in both ways is part of the strict procedure of Coordinate Remote Viewing. You need to be able to do it each way in order to have a fuller sense of the target. Liking one method more than the other simply allows you to know which way you are more comfortable with receiving the information and which one you need to work on. But there is no right or wrong answer—good job!

It's a Wrap!

Whichever way you prefer is not really important. What is important is that you stick to the process. The procedure, as done up until now, is crucial to this final step. By gathering all of the data from the target site, you should have a pretty clear idea of what the coordinates you were given mean. At the very least, you may think you know what they are and it's now time to jump into the next step of preparing a viewer's summary.

This is the final part of Coordinate Remote Viewing. The viewer's summary does not negate the rest of the session. In fact, it should add to it. More often than not, the summary will reflect the information received during the remote examination of the target data. For instance, if you were summarizing the movie theater in the example above, you may have written down the title of a scary movie that was playing during your viewing. Or, you may have listed a few different movies as a way to tap into the target area during its normal state.

You might find that as you are summarizing your CRV session, one or more of your AOLs or AOL/Ss come into your synopsis and either add to or detract from what you believe the target site to be. Whatever comes to mind, as before, is what you should be writing down. If the AOLs jump in, that's fine. If not, that's okay as well.

Interestingly, however, you may find that your summary identifies something entirely different than what you thought you were viewing during all of the various stages throughout your CRV session. For example, you may think you are at a cruise ship, but are instead are at the Crystal Mosque, as was the case earlier. But if you look at the session summary used in that example, you will find the data to be accurate—the conclusion, however, was wrong. Alternatively, you may have been writing down cruise ship information all the way through the viewing, but during the summary you write that it was, indeed, the Crystal Mosque, or at least some sort of mosque.

Try It Now!

Summarizing the Movie

Using the movie theater example again, write a summary of your viewing. What are you writing down? Are you including the details of the seats? Are there curtains around the movie screen? Is it dark or light? Is it loud or quiet? Do you hear music? Do you smell popcorn? Record everything here in the summary by putting it in sentence format using the following as a prompter:

"I am in the target area. Around me I see/hear/taste/touch/ feel/sense _____."

How does it feel to write it like this? Does it make you feel more in control of where you are? More confused? Is it easier or harder than recording the descriptive data you've previously used? If someone were to read your summary, would they know right away where you are?

Completing the six stages of Coordinate Remote Viewing enables you to get out there and practice on target sites. If you are so inclined, you can re-do the exercises from part two until you are not just performing them as you read, but also learning a process that you can walk away with and do on your own or even with other viewers. Remember, practicing will help to reinforce the method and can make the process feel more natural.

Learning how to combine your remote viewing skills with your psychic sight is coming up next. Absorbing the knowledge to work with both will put you on a whole new level!

Part Three

PRACTICE & PRACTICAL USE

"If at first you don't succeed, try, try again."
—W.E. Hickson

Chapter Thirteen
Making It Work for You

By now, you've worked with your natural and developing clairvoyance. You've also learned about the strict process of Coordinate Remote Viewing. Hopefully, you've reaped the benefits of each distinctly different method. While reading the book, and as you've done the various exercises, you've probably felt drawn to one practice more than the other. This is very typical and something that can be expected. A few of you may feel an almost equal pull to both methods, but that is rare. Using your left as well as your right brain functions, the creative space and the logical space, can help to balance you out, and that's what may happen if you're feeling comfortable with both methods. If you're like me, you need that balance!

Working It Together

Working with your psychic vision and Coordinate Remote Viewing can be kept as separate activities or can be combined. Either one can become the adjunct function, or they can both be equally important. Each type of viewing has its benefits and neither should be discarded as uninformative or useless. Usually, circumstances will determine which method will work better or better fits the situation, or if a combination is necessary. It also becomes a judgment based on what you feel is just the right way to go.

Using clairvoyance, for example, can give you an overall feeling or understanding of something, while CRV can be used to give a more specific location or event. Or, remote viewing can help you locate something that's missing, while psychic abilities can help fill in the blanks and make the target data less hollow, more detailed and distinct.

I have been faced with the dilemma of figuring out which mode to use a few times while doing psychic investigative work for families with missing or murdered loved ones. Each circumstance required me to tune in to their loved ones. I had to choose which way to do that. Instead of discounting one method and only using the other, I decided to utilize both of my methods. By using my psychic abilities as well as my remote viewing training, I was able to gain a deeper understanding of the circumstances leading to and surrounding their loved ones. Each method afforded me a different perspective and gave me information that I may have missed otherwise.

For example, for one session, while using my psychic abilities I saw my dock at my lake house. This I interpreted to be symbolic, as the missing person was actually in a completely different country. This clairvoyant image meant the person was near or in the water. By using remote viewing after that, I was able to pinpoint a more accurate location of the actual body of water. In another session, I used remote viewing and landed in the actual crime scene. I was able to see the events leading up to the person's murder. I then tuned in clairvoyantly to the person and his place of employment and where he lived by seeing actual signage in my mind's eye. I was also able to get a pretty good idea of what kind of person he was and who he associated with, which showed me he was just in the wrong place at the wrong time. Unfortunately, it had been a case of mistaken identity.

By using psychic sight as well as remote viewing I was able to get a more accurate picture of what had happened in each circumstance. Though these are extreme examples, they show not only how one modality can be used with the other, but also that they can actually enhance each other.

Clairvoyance and Coordinate Remote Viewing can also be used together in a less intense manner to find lost or missing objects. This was the case when Grace came in for a reading. I connected psychically to her deceased loved ones on the other side. During the reading I had asked her, "What happened to the jewelry?"

"Wow! I was going to ask *you* that!" she replied.

I had seen gold rings, necklaces, and bracelets with my clairvoyance, my psychic vision. But then I saw them disappear. This told me they were missing.

"These are from your loved ones, part of what was left to you when the passed," I continued.

"Yes, exactly! I can't find them, though! Do you know where they are?"

I tuned in, using my training in remote viewing, and went through a quick, shortened version of the process. What I saw made sense.

"I believe they are in a drawer, in your living room, in a flowered bag." I also went on to tell her, "I think you put them there so you wouldn't lose them!"

She laughed. "That would be me! Putting them somewhere and then forgetting where I put them!"

My psychic vision had come through for her. Later that week she let me know she had indeed found them in her living room, in a flowered bag, in a drawer. She was ecstatic. These pieces were about more than their monetary value, they were special. Using clairvoyance and remote viewing had helped make her day. This is something you can learn to do for yourself. The more often you work with each modality, the more familiar you will become with them, and the more comfortable you will be combining them.

Group Viewing

One of the things I love best about teaching and even taking classes is that I can always feel the energy in the room being raised. With more people connecting to their higher power and directing their clairvoyant gifts to open, accessing the psychic information can be easier. When Coordinate Remote Viewing is used as well as psychic vision, more people interpreting the target allows for a greater picture of exactly what it is you are looking at. Working together as a group, as in many of life's pursuits, can give you fuller, more enhanced representation of the information you are seeing.

Share this information with your friends and practice together. Have them get their own copy of this book for reference, or share with them. (Though experience tells me you won't want to give away your copy!) You may even find yourself developing a remote viewing group or club. In the psychic world we call this a Circle. It's simply the forming of a group of like-minded individuals who come together to work on developing their abilities in a positive way. You are among the lucky ones who have now been exposed to both types of remote viewing and can therefore participate and share more fully with others.

As you proceed with the group viewing process you'll need to decide which type of group it will be: psychic, or remote viewing, or whether you will alternate. It is important, as if you didn't already know, to maintain the structure of remote viewing, so you want to be sure to follow the strict protocol. With psychic vision it's a bit different. I don't mean it's a free-for-all, but it definitely leaves room for variation from person to person and even for each person's preferred methods. You may find that some favor tuning in to their clairvoyant gifts through meditation and some do it more through psychometry. However you choose to tune in is fine, as long as you do it with the correct intentions.

With a psychic circle, you can proceed in many different directions or you can choose to change it up with each meeting. You can have everyone work together on a specific target or everyone can do their own thing. Psychometry is great for this. Having each person bring an object, such as a piece of jewelry or a picture, can help you practice. By swapping the items randomly and blindly, you can all write down anything you psychically see or say out loud what you're seeing with your third eye. This is a great way to practice.

When using Coordinate Remote Viewing to gather information on targets while in a group, you need to allow for one person be the moderator. So, for example, say you have five people in your group. Four should be prepared to actually do the viewing and one should be the person who presents the others with the coordinates. This is also the person who begins the session and ends the session. Group sessions are often limited so that all can begin and end at the same time. The moderator then would collect all the data the viewers gathered and compare their notes. By connecting the information, you will get a broader perspective on the target site. Above all, again, it should be something that you work together as a group to do.

In general, the group experience should elevate your ability to tune in, no matter which method. If this doesn't happen, form a different group or look for an existing one. It should also be enjoyable. This is never supposed to be viewed as something you have to do, but rather something you love doing. Forming a group may take some time, and you may have to search to find like-minded people, but eventually they will show up. Also, as mentioned, you may want to try to search out other groups that are already formed. There are remote viewing groups on the Internet as well as psychic practice groups. You'd be amazed at the knowledge and data you can gain even when others in the group are in different countries!

Practice May Make Perfect

Practice makes perfect. Okay, so maybe not perfect, but as close to it as possible! This chapter will expose you to multiple targets and messages to practice on. You'll be able to access them through Coordinate Remote Viewing as well as your psychic vision. Enjoy the process!

For these practice targets, there will be three with specific coordinates for you to use your Coordinate Remote Viewing skills with. Others without coordinates will be listed as Target A, B, or C. For these, you can use your clairvoyance. Having said that, you are welcome to practice on all of them both ways. Just be sure you don't check the target feedback at the end of the book before completing them using both methods, or you will cheat yourself of the opportunity to practice.

Before you begin, it is crucial to have multiple pens and lots of paper handy. Use blank paper, such as copy paper, and make sure you have plenty. You won't want to interrupt yourself because you need to go find more while you're in the middle of a session. Don't use a journal for this. You can always punch holes in the papers and insert them into a notebook afterward, but you want blank, flat paper to work with your practice targets so you can move them around and go back when necessary. You also don't want any bindings or fasteners in your way as you are working.

Remember, with Coordinate Remote Viewing you may decide you want to stop before Stage IV. That is perfectly acceptable. If you decide to do that for these practice targets, be sure to continue on to your written summary. The session will not be concluded or finished until that is done.

With your psychic vision, follow the same process as you did in this book. Tune in to all of your clair senses and allow messages to come through. Record whatever symbols you receive and explain what they may mean. Ask the basic questions about the target: who, what, where, when, how, why. Allow yourself to fully expand on them. As with Coordinate Remote Viewing, finish your session by writing a summary. Remember, this is not a guess about your target data; it is instead based on what and how you feel and what you saw with your psychic abilities.

The feedback for all of the practice targets is at the end of the book. Again, don't cheat yourself! Wait until you're done practicing, at least one at a time, before you look at the answers. You want to give yourself the chance to succeed and even excel at this as you go. With all the targets, the feedback presented is very basic. Please feel free to look up and gather additional data in order to give yourself as much information on the target as possible. Looking at a variety of pictures, from multiple angles, may help to validate the data you've recorded.

This is practice. It should be fun. Good luck and enjoy!

Review of CRV to Work with Target Data

Here is a quick review of the process of Coordinate Remote Viewing to help you work with your target data:

Begin with your name, date, ST, and ET
Advanced Visuals?
Physical or Personal Inclemency?

Stage I:
Write down the coordinates
Draw your ideogram
Work the ideogram
> *A. Motion component*
> *B. Manmade or natural*
> *C. Structure, mountain, water, land, land/water interface, or life form*

Reminder of breaks:
> *Analytical overlay (AOL)*
> *AOL Drive*
> *Confusion*
> *Too Much (TM)*
> *Personal Inclemency (PI)*
> *Missed*
> *Bi Location (BI)*
> *Emotional Impact (EI)*
> *Aesthetic Impact (AI)*

Stage II:
> *Sensory data*
> *Dimensionals*
> *Sketch*

Stage III:
> *Movement*
> *Draw it more, center stage*

Stage IV:
> *Matrix chart—one column at a time*

Stage V:
> *Cognitrons*
>> *Objects*
>> *Attributes*
>> *Subject*
>> *Topics*

Stage VI:
> *Build a model*
> *Matrix chart—chaotic*

Summarize it!

Coordinate Remote Viewing Target Coordinates:
2014
6724

2014
0813

1696
4597

Review of Clairvoyance
to View Your Targets

Here is a quick review of the methods you can use to tune in to your clair-voyance to view your targets. Remember, though, everyone will come to use their own procedure in order to tune in once your groups become comfortable enough with it. These suggestions, though important, are based on tried and true practices I have used!

Close your eyes and breathe
Protect yourself
Connect to your imagination
Pay attention to any physical cues
Allow visions to flow
Employ your other psychic gifts, the other clairs
Try psychometry, hold the coordinates
Pay attention to any symbols & interpret according to your personal feeling

Psychic Vision/Clairvoyant Targets:

A

B

C

"Don't try to comprehend with your mind.
Your minds are very limited. Use your intuition."
—Madeleine L'Engle

Chapter Fourteen
Wrapping It Up!

No Limits

You've been given an extraordinary opportunity most never have. The knowledge you've gained is cause enough to celebrate! You now have insight into a world that you may have never known about had you not only witnessed it but been part of it yourself. You've tapped into your intuition and you've learned to work with a protocol that government spies used. Just the thought of that is incredible. Your life, whether you expected it or not, is now changed forever. As gifted intuitive Dr. Mona Lisa Schulz said in her book *Awakening Intuition: Using Your Mind-Body Network for Insight and Healing,* "Intuition inspires us to become creative in our lives and in the ways we view our lives."

As incredible as it is, you may still experience a bit of frustration, because as you develop your remote viewing abilities you may feel limited at times. You can absolutely do anything you want, so why should you have to feel limited in any way? This is not about self-imposed limitations or even limitations placed on your remote viewing abilities by others at all. Rather, this is about accepting that you may not receive the exact detailed messages you are hoping for. Often the signs and communications we receive leave many blanks to be filled in. Sometimes learning how to understand these gaps in psychic visions can be as crucial to the clairvoyant messages as the impressions themselves. Do not pigeonhole yourself and create limitations. You've got everything you need to succeed.

As a professional psychic, I am faced with this dilemma every day. When people come in they are often specifically looking for me to validate a certain area of their life. Now, while this is a common occurrence, it is not guaranteed that I will always automatically tune in to why they are there or what they do. I believe this is partly due to limiting beliefs. What one person thinks of as their main contribution or their gift in life may not be what the reading will bring through. Everyone has many gifts, many things to offer the world. This reinforces the fact that you should not limit yourself to what you believe your current label should be.

I did a reading for someone the other day. Very stoic, she came in with a challenging air. Though to ask her if she was guarded and challenging would have brought a litany of protest. But during the reading, every time I'd tell her something she didn't want to hear, she would show me her disapproval by saying, "Let's just move on." And if I told her something she'd already somewhat hinted at, she'd tell me, "I just told you that." So at the very end, when she said, "I'm surprised you didn't pick up on my healing abilities," I had to tell her she'd already hinted at it so there was no reason for me to reiterate it. This seemed to shock her, that I hadn't mentioned what she was so good at. But as I said, there is so much more to everyone, and sometimes it's the ego that needs stroking rather than the gift that needs mentioning.

Knowing that you will not always share exactly what someone may be looking for, or even being aware that you may not tune in directly to the target data but might instead focus on the area around the target, will allow you the opportunity to not always have to be perfect or perfectly correct. Knowing we are all, as humans and individuals, occasionally limited but still have the capacity to soar, lets you explore without limiting your reach. We have unlimited potential to be who and what we want. Our genius is in our intuitive mind.

Whether through email, phone calls, or in person, one of the most common questions I receive is, "How do I get more information?" This comes from people who are doing both Coordinate Remote Viewing and clairvoyantly tuning in. I answer with what seems like a simplistic, almost nonchalant answer: "Ask." That's it. Sounds easy, right? Yet it always works. Just ask. Ask the universe to help you get the answers you are looking for, or even to know what to look for. Whether you are trying to fill in the blanks or search for more information for yourself or your client, remember to ask for what you need.

Try It Now!

Just Ask for It!

Take a moment to think back to all of the exercises you have already done. Were there any that left you wanting more? Do you think that you could have added to what you saw psychically or with your Coordinate Remote Viewing if you had opened yourself up to the universe and asked for more? If so, when would you have asked? What blanks do you feel you may have been able to fill in? Would you have received more details?

Review your previous exercises and pick one to perform again. This time, ask for more when you feel like you are either not getting enough information or need to fill in where something may be missing. Are you able to receive more than you did the first time you did the exercise? Less? Did it feel natural to ask for additional data? Try another exercise if you'd like to explore this some more!

It's your turn now, to learn for yourself. As a professional, it's very encouraging to have clients come in who are not only looking to me for answers but who also want to learn how to develop their own gifts, their own intuitive abilities. This, almost as much as giving readings, is what I love to do. When that metaphoric lightbulb goes off over someone's head, I can feel their energy, their excitement, and it reignites my passion to share my knowledge and wisdom with them and assist them in welcoming their psychic senses. There is something inherently comforting in being able to see, psychically, how something will play out or which path leads to the pot of gold. It's a natural gift, our sixth sense to receive intuitive messages, and once we discover that, there's really no turning it off.

Once you've opened the door to psychically and remotely see for yourself, you'll find yourself presented with opportunities to see for others as well. Comforting others is also a significant part of developing your clairvoyant gifts. This happened with my friend Katie. She has been interested in psychic phenomena for quite a while and is always excited to tune in when possible. She shared with me an experience she had recently regarding an acquaintance, Barbara, who had passed. Though she didn't know Barbara well—she had been the mother of a friend of Katie's daughter—Katie was clearly the conduit for bringing Barbara's family comfort.

Comfort for Others

Dreams are a very common way to have clairvoyant images come through. Mainly this is because we don't judge and push them away, as our subconscious mind is really doing the work (versus our conscious mind) while we sleep. This was a normal modality by which Katie received visitations from the other side. Psychic awareness, remember, can come through mediumship, which occurs regularly during our nightly slumber.

Barbara appeared to Katie in full form, clearly and beautifully, to ask Katie to convey a message to her family that she was okay. Katie was quite concerned about this because she didn't really know the family, so she asked for a sign. She wanted clarification that she was indeed supposed to relay the message. She asked to see Barbara's mother or sister, and then she would share Barbara's visit with them.

Less than forty-five minutes later, while walking out of a wake for a different family friend, she walked right into Barbara's mom. Shaken and not feeling entirely confident, she decided it was not the right time to explain what had happened. Again, she believed she would be given another chance. So, she found the address and went to Barbara's parents' home later that day. Though she felt a bit awkward, she also knew she was being propelled to follow through by Barbara.

When the father answered the door, he too felt he needed to let her in, and as they waited for Barbara's mom to return home, Katie shared her message for the family. She said she just had to tell them Barbara was okay. When the mother returned, she was ecstatic. They too had asked for a sign that their departed daughter was all right, and here it was. Katie trusted that her clairvoyant vision, even though it occured during her dream, was true and that the sign she had asked for was given to her. She knew it was meaningful, and luckily she went with her intuition and brought peace and comfort to Barbara's family.

Learning to trust what comes through can take time, but it is worth the effort. Whether you use your gifts for yourself or for others, there's a reason you have them and can develop them. Look at it this way—if you could help someone, why would you hold back? Knowing you have the power to comfort yourself or others can be enough of a driving force to propel you forward. Besides that, tuning in psychically or with remote viewing is just plain awesome!

Now Get Out There!

There's a time and a place for psychic vision or Coordinate Remote Viewing. To help divine the future, or to find someone who is lost, or even to locate a missing item—these are all perfect times to use your gifts. Learning how to do this and which method to use will allow you to facilitate the experiences for others and yourself in a way that really proves valuable.

You are ready! Go out and do readings for anyone and everyone! All right, maybe not, but you have learned so much. Take advantage of everything you've done up to this point and use it to build on your budding psychic abilities. Throughout this book, you've accessed your third eye and seen images you may never have seen before. You've also discovered how science truly does mesh with the paranormal through the use of Coordinate Remote Viewing. You've gained knowledge through practice and become more aware of how frequent and how accurate your psychic abilities actually are. You have reintroduced yourself to your psychic birthright.

Live for the moment instead of living in the past. I recently posted something on social media: "Kangaroos cannot physically jump backward. We should take a cue from them and stop reliving the past. Instead, use our energy in the present, and move forward as we progress naturally." Worrying about whether or not you are good enough or if you did a good reading or did something wrong will get you nowhere.

Live now. Don't live with one foot in the past. And don't live in the future. Live in the present. We worry about tomorrow like it's guaranteed. There is nothing that says tomorrow will come. Focus on today. Do not focus on how right you are—that will inevitably set you up for failure. Take advantage of the opportunities you have to practice and hone your skills, whether your slant is more toward psychic or scientific remote viewing.

There's nothing holding you back. You have everything you need to move forward. You may have realized by now that you are more drawn to one method over the other. You may also have noticed that you enjoy learning and working with both methods. My hope for you is that you have gained enough wisdom to feel somewhat comfortable with each of the techniques.

Still not sure what to do or where it can take you? The answer is simple. Listening to your intuition will tell you everything you need to know. You have merely touched the tip of the iceberg. There is so much more out there for you to explore. The boundaries you've currently set for yourself were once uncharted territory. You've already come so far and have so many opportunities to go even further. Enjoy your new skills and use them wisely—they will bring you to places most people will never go!

Target Feedback

Coordinate Remote Viewing

Target feedback:
2014
6734

What is it? Batman: The Ride, a Roller Coaster
Where is it? Great Adventure, Six Flags, in Jackson, NJ
When is it? 2014

Other relevant information:
Top speed: 50 mph
Elevation: 105 feet
Length: 2693 feet
Duration: 1 minute 40 seconds
Manufacturer: B & M

Target feedback:
2014
0813

What is it? My office
Where is it? Center for Healing, 77 Danbury Road, Ridgefield, CT 06877
When is it? August 13, 2014

Other relevant information:
Office use: Client sessions—readings, coaching, hypnosis, writing, etc.
Other: Phone sessions, group events, workshops, orange walls, and antique furniture
Remainder of office space: Waiting room, two other therapists' offices

Target Feedback:
   1696
   4597

What is it? The Great Sphinx of Giza
Where is it? Giza, Egypt

Other relevant data:
Other landmarks: Great Pyramids of Giza, Nile River
Tourist attraction—date of build unknown
(though head is possibly Pharaoh Khafra, who reigned sometime between 2400 BC and 2700 BC)

Mythological creature—body of a lion, head of man

Psychic Vision

Target Feedback:
A
What is it? Eiffel Tower
Where is it? On the Champ de Mars, Paris, France
When is it? Current

Other relevant data:
Built in 1889 by Gustave Eiffel as the entrance to the 1889 World's Fair
324 meters tall/1,063 feet tall, metal structure
Tower has three levels, restaurants, and observatory

Target Feedback:
B
What is it? Michael Jackson
When is it? August 29, 1958–June 25, 2009

Other relevant information:
Known as the King of Pop, greatest selling album of all time
Winner of multiple awards, including thirteen Grammys, Grammy
Legend & Lifetime Achievement Awards, 26 American Music Awards

Born in Gary, Indiana, United States
Performer since childhood, Jackson 5

Target Feedback:
C
What is it? Daytona 500 NASCAR Sprint Cup Race
When is it? Annual race, 1959–present
Where is it? Daytona Beach, Florida, Daytona International Speedway

Other relevant data:
500-mile race, 200 laps, NASCAR Sprint Cars
Richard Petty, driver with most wins overall (7)
Winner receives Harley J. Earl Trophy
Adjacent museum & gallery

Glossary

Aesthetic Impact: How the target makes the viewer feel; a subjective emotional response from the viewer to the site

Analytical Overlay (AOL): Analytical, intellectual, or psychic belief about what the target is; having a false sense of the target due to the mind's need to analyze the signal line data

Chakra(s): Metaphysical energy centers or spiritual batteries through which life force or *chi* moves; the centers of spiritual power where energy flows from and to the aura

Clair(s): French word meaning "clear," representing clear psychic abilities; the prefix for the extrasensory abilities words, i.e., clairvoyance

Clairalience: Psychic ability related to scent; the ability to psychically smell something

Clairaudience: Psychic ability related to hearing; the ability to psychically hear something

Claircognizance: Psychic ability where you just know something without knowing why or where the knowledge came from; being conscious of something for no known reason

Clairempathy: Experiencing a psychic emotion toward someone or something; feeling an actual emotion in response to a psychic connection

Clairescence: Psychic ability related to scent; the ability to psychically smell something

Clairgustance: Psychic ability related to taste; the ability to psychically taste something

Clairolfaction: Psychic ability related to scent; the ability to psychically smell something

Clairsentience: Psychic ability where you feel in your body or your senses; feeling something in your gut; intuitive hunches

Clairtangency: Gaining information psychically through touch; psychically tuning in to an object or person when touching

Clairvoyance: *See also* Intuitive, Psychic, Psychic Abilities, Psychic Sight, and Psychic Vision: Psychic ability related to sight; the ability to psychically see something using your third eye

Cognitron: Groups of neurons that have come together to form an idea or concept; a group or cluster of elements that make up a concept; neurons which, when joined together with the synapses, produce a fuller final concept

Coordinate Remote Viewing (CRV): *See also* Remote Viewing: A term coined by Stanford Research Institute (SRI) International to describe a specific protocol designed to induce a trained ability to obtain accurate data from persons, places, things, and events distant in both time and space; a method that can be taught for gathering information from a target distant in time and space that has been assigned random numbered coordinates

Coordinates: A random set of numbers assigned with the intent to represent a specific target at a time specified

Dimensionals: Listing in Stage II which uses single (occasionally double) words to describe the dimensions of the target; basic dimensionals may include height, width, depth, and size

Energetics: Single words used to describe the energy of or at the target site; basic energetics may include bouncing, pulsing, shaking, buzzing

Extrasensory: Referring to the psychic senses beyond the basic five physical senses

Group Viewing: A group of like-minded people generally focusing and viewing the same target data, blind to each other's intelligence during the session

Guides: Messengers from the other side who assist us by delivering messages we can intuitively or psychically interpret

I/A/B/C: I=Ideogram, A=Motion of ideogram, B=Natural or manmade, C=structure, mountain, water, land, land/water interface, or life form.

Ideogram: An automatic line drawing induced by writing down the coordinates in the beginning of a remote viewing session; the initial connection to the signal line in order to access the target data

Imagination: The ability to visualize images, pictures, objects, or thoughts in your mind that are not real; making up something that is not real in your mind; the creative space in your mind that forms images from scratch

Intuition: *See also* Intuitive, Psychic, Psychic Abilities: Gut instinct or instinctive knowledge; something you believe without having proof or evidence; a sixth sense which guides you; psychic ability

Intuitive: *See also* Intuitive, Psychic, Psychic Abilities: Possessing intuition; using what one feels to be true without evidence or conscious reasoning

Matrix: A framework of information accessible to everyone, connected to everything, everyone, and every moment in time, from which the signal line emerges; also referred to as universal energy or the collective unconsciousness

Premonition: Having psychic or intuitive knowledge of an event before it occurs

Prophetic: To describe or accurately predict what is to come or what will happen in the future with no evidence; to prophesy or tell of something

Psychic: The ability to know things through extrasensory perception

Psychic Abilities: Various extrasensory gifts which allow you to know things

Psychic Sight: *See also* Clairvoyance: Clairvoyant; psychically seeing with your third eye; seeing images in your mind without the use of your physical eyes

Psychic Vision: *See also* Psychic Sight, Clairvoyance: also, the act of seeing psychically

Reading: Giving someone information that you gain through psychic methods, often in a counselor/client situation

Remote Viewing: *See also* Coordinate Remote Viewing: The act of seeing something distant in time and space

Senses: Psychic receptors of information, providing data for perception

Sign: Extrasensory or paranormal external messages from the other side; physical object which shows up to answer questions or to guide us in the right direction

Symbol: Message sent from the other side to symbolize or represent something; impression psychically received from the other side

Synchronicity: A series of seemingly unrelated events which, when recognized, holds meaning; often referred to as coincidence

Target: *See also* Target Data: A location, person, thing, or event distant in time and space that is to be viewed

Target Data: *See also* Target: The information gained from remote viewing a target

Third Eye: Clairvoyant energy center; the sixth chakra, located in the center of the forehead; the chakra used for psychic sight

Bibliography and Recommended Reading

Alvarez, Melissa. *Your Psychic Self: A Quick and Easy Guide to Discovering Your Intuitive Talents.* Woodbury, MN: Llewellyn Publications, 2013.

Choquette, Sonia. *Trust Your Vibes: Secret Tools for Six-Sensory Living.* Carlsbad, CA: Hay House, 2004.

Firedocs Remote Viewing –Archives- TOC and Links, Palyne "PJ" Gaenir, 11/301/2104, http://www.firedocs.com/remoteviewing/

Hewitt, William W. *Psychic Development for Beginners: An Easy Guide to Developing & Releasing Your Psychic Abilities.* St. Paul, MN: Llewellyn Publications, 1996.

Hicks, Abraham. www.youtube.com/watch?v=34A5w7hWny8. 3/13/2011.

http://www.firedocs.com/remoteviewing/answers/crvmanual/smith01.html

http://www.firedocs.com/remoteviewing/answers/crvmanual/swann01.html

Koppel, Ted. "Psychic Spies." *ABC Nightline News.* November 28, 1995.

Llewis, Clive Staples. *The Collected Letters of C. S. Lewis.* San Francisco: Harper, 2005.

McMoneagle, Joseph. *Remote Viewing Secrets.* Charlottesville, VA: Hampton Roads Publishing, 2000.

———. *Memoirs of a Psychic Spy: The Remarkable Life of U.S. Government Remote Viewer 001*. Charlottesville, VA: Hampton Roads Publishing, 2006.

Morehouse, David. *Coordinate Remote Viewing Training Manual, Version Nine*. San Marcos, CA: Remote Viewing Technologies International, 2003.

———. *Psychic Warrior: Inside the CIA's Stargate Program: The True Story of a Soldier's Espionage and Awakening*. New York: St. Martin's Press, 1996.

Schulz, Mona Lisa, MD, PhD. *Awakening Intuition: Using Your Mind-Body Network for Insight and Healing*. New York: Harmony Press, 1998.

Smith, Daz. "About Remote Viewing." http://www.remoteviewed.com/about_remote_viewing.htm.

Targ, Russel, PhD, Harold Puthoff, PhD, Ingo Swann, Paul Smith, Major, Retired US Army, Skip (Fred) Atwater. *DIA Remote Viewing Training Manual*. Defense Intelligence Agency (DIA) & Stanford Research Institute International. Menlo Park, CA, 1986.

Todeschi, Kevin. *The Encyclopedia of Symbolism*. New York: Berkley Publishing Group, 1995.

Van Praagh, James. *Heaven and Earth: Making the Psychic Connection*. New York: Simon & Schuster, 2001.

Additional Target Resources

Controlled Remote Viewing, http://www.crviewer.com/targets/target-index.php

David Morehouse Productions, http://davidmorehouse.com/practice-targets/

The Western Institute of Remote Viewing, http://www.remoteviewers.com/htms/updated/target_instructions/target.htm

Index

To Write to the Author

If you wish to contact the author or would like more information about this book, please write to the author in care of Llewellyn Worldwide and we will forward your request. Both the author and publisher appreciate hearing from you and learning of your enjoyment of this book and how it has helped you. Llewellyn Worldwide cannot guarantee that every letter written to the author can be answered, but all will be forwarded. Please write to:

Melanie Barnum
℅ Llewellyn Worldwide Ltd.
2143 Wooddale Drive
Woodbury, MN 55125-2989

Please enclose a self-addressed stamped envelope for reply,
or $1.00 to cover costs. If outside the U.S.A., enclose
an international postal reply coupon.

Many of Llewellyn's authors have websites with additional information and resources. For more information, please visit our website at http://www.llewellyn.com.